MW01611363

Coaching Soccer Through Small-Sided Games

Let the Game be the Teacher with 101 Small-Sided Games

Published by
WORLD CLASS COACHING

First published September, 2007 by
WORLD CLASS COACHING 15004 Buena Vista Drive, Leawood, KS 66224
(913) 402-0030

ISBN 0-9788936-5-1
Copyright © WORLD CLASS COACHING 2007

Edited by Tom Mura

Cover Design: Mark Palmer - p2 creative

Published by
WORLD CLASS COACHING

Table of Contents

Introduction

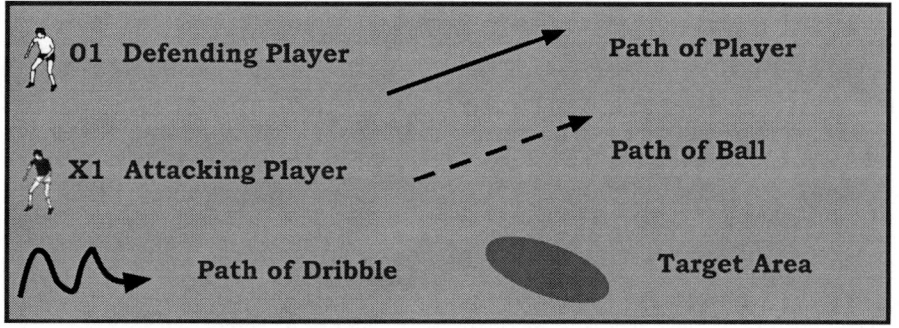

Introduction

One of the most important components of a training session is the 'small-sided game'. Whether it's a local youth team, college team or a top professional team, they all use small-sided games to help their players make the transition from drills and exercises to real game situations. It's this transition that translates skills and techniques from practice into your game on the weekend.

Coaching Soccer through Small-Sided Games contains 101 games that incorporate a wide range of topics including: Passing and Possession, Shooting, Crossing and Finishing, Defending, Half Field Games and Full Field Games. Small-sided games are a great way to focus on these topics in a game-like situation. Another benefit of incorporating small-sided games into your training sessions is that players enjoy them.

Many of the small-sided games in this book are taken from the last 10 years of the WORLD CLASS COACHING magazine and are from the training sessions of some of the world's top teams and coaches including: Manchester United, Real Madrid, AC Milan, Juventus, Liverpool, U.S Women's World Cup Team, and from world-renowned coaches like Tony DiCicco and others make this book a must have for any serious soccer coach.

Chapter One

Warm-Up

This game is from an article that was written by Dave Clarke, Head Women's Coach at Quinnipiac University in Connecticut. The notes were provided by Martin Tierney of www.Soccerexperience.com. England National Team Training Session - June 1, 2001 La Manga, Spain, six days before a World Cup qualifier against Greece in Athens.

Warm-Up

The team splits into two groups, one with bibs and one with no bibs. The players jog anywhere on the field without a ball, occasionally stopping for individual stretching.

After 6-7 minutes they come back into the coaches, but only Sammy Lee speaks to the players. The players continue the warm-up in pairs, working on various types of ball control with the service out of the hand. After stopping for a group stretch, they continue to work with the same partner while passing and moving all over the field.

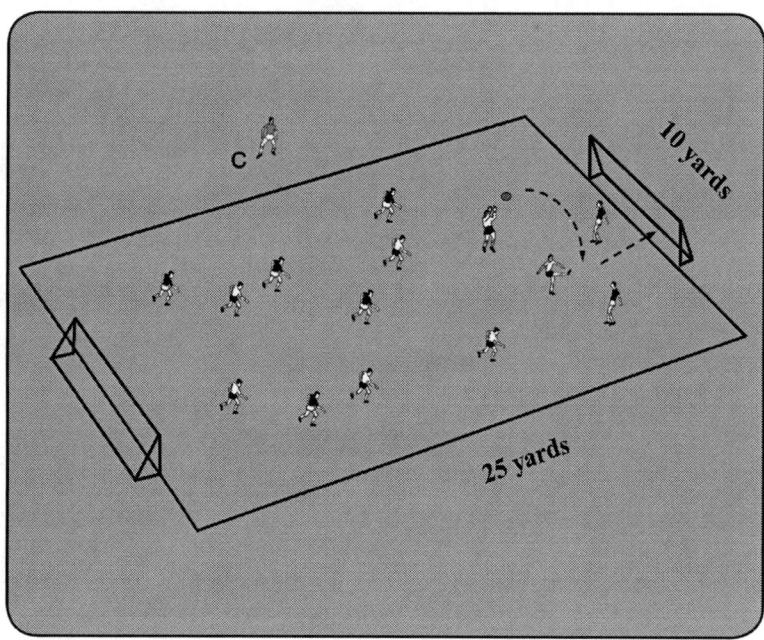

*This game was observed during a visit to the Crystal Palace Youth Academy.
There I observed the training sessions of the U11, U15 and U16 teams. The
training session was done in the evening, outdoors on an artificial surface.
The weather was windy with the temperature close to freezing.*

U11 Possession Game

Play 6 v 6 possession in a 30 x 20-yard area. A player is positioned on both
of the 30-yard perimeter lines. The players inside the grid can pass to the
perimeter players if they wish. The perimeter players can move along their
line looking to receive a pass and play the ball back into the grid but they
must avoid taking too long to make the pass.

Progressions
• Perimeter player can dribble the ball in and change places with the player
  that passed to him
• Play directional

Coaching Point
When the inside player receives a pass from the perimeter player, he should
look to open up and see if he can turn.

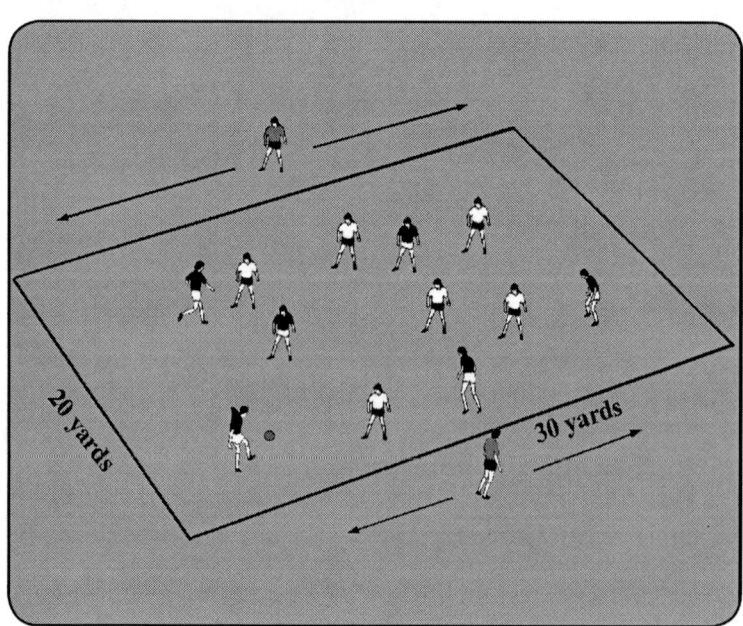

Progression
Increase the area to 30 x 30 yards and place small goals, cones or flags at both ends. This time the players are playing directional and attempting to score.

Coaching Point
Look to switch play

Practice ended with a 30-minute scrimmage.

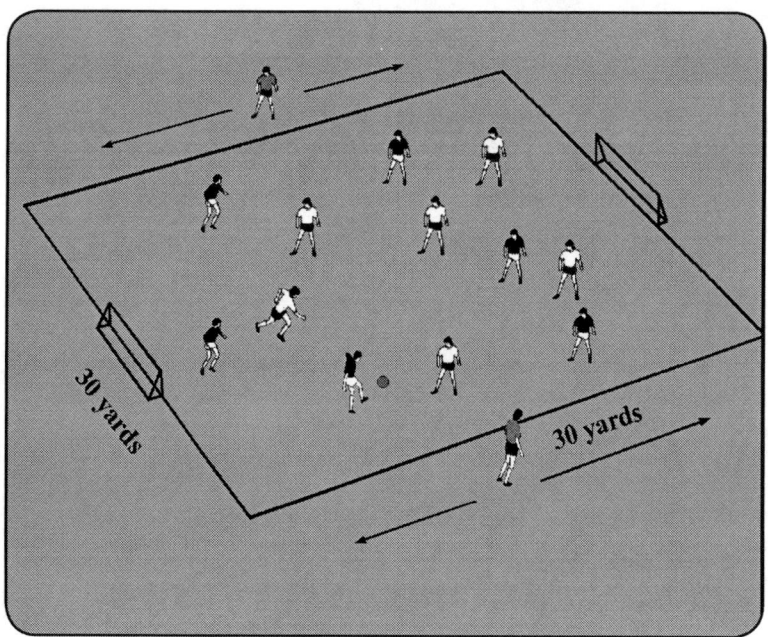

Chapter Two
Passing & Possession

Tom Goodman is the former US Youth Soccer Director of Coaching Education. Goodman holds a USSF 'A' License and a USSF National Youth License. His many soccer positions have included US Soccer Region I National Staff Coach, USYSA Region 1 Staff Coach, and a member of the Board of Directors for the NSCAA. This warm-up was part of a session that was observed at the 2003 NSCAA Convention in Kansas City and was demonstrated using the U15 Kansas City Pace team.

Exercise Five: Make It-Take It

Play 4 v 4 + 1 with the objective of passing the ball into the goalkeepers' (who are situated in end zones) hands.

Coaching Points
- Introduce the concept of shape: width and depth of the field
- Encourage players to play the way they are facing
- Wide players should open up appropriately
- Work on playing direct soccer

Progression
Increase the number of players, the size of the field and introduce full sized goals.

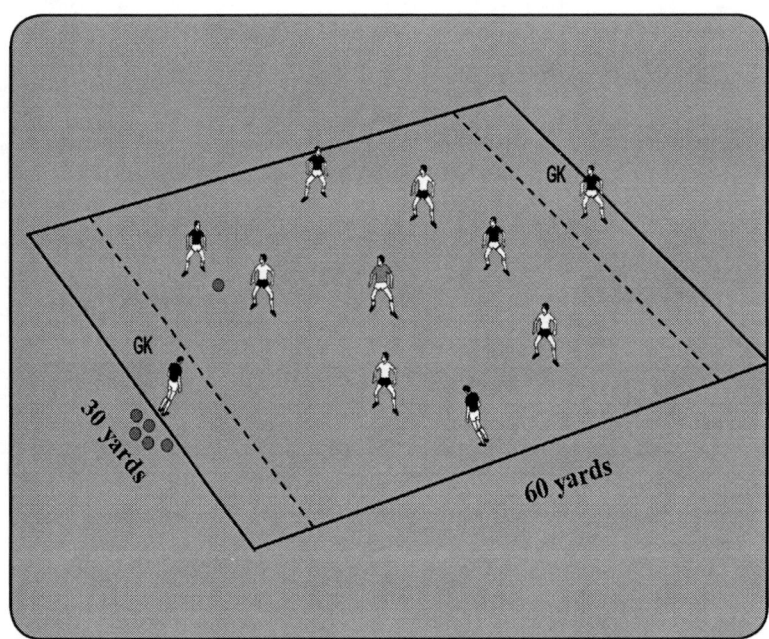

These games were part of a session is submitted by Brian Matzke. Brian currently coaches with the West Hartford Girls Soccer Club in Connecticut. The session was in preparation for A.C. Milan's Champions World Series game against Manchester United in August 2004. The session lasted roughly 90 minutes and involved 16 field players and three goalkeepers.

8 v 6 Keep-Away

Mark a field with cones approximately 10 yards in from each touchline and three yards in from the halfway line and edge of penalty area. Play with two teams with one having a numerical advantage (8 v 6). Play using one or two touches. There is very little dribbling. Play focuses through the middle of the field. The game speed is below regular game pace. The main focus is on forcing the team with the ball, to maintain possession with quick passing and combination play.

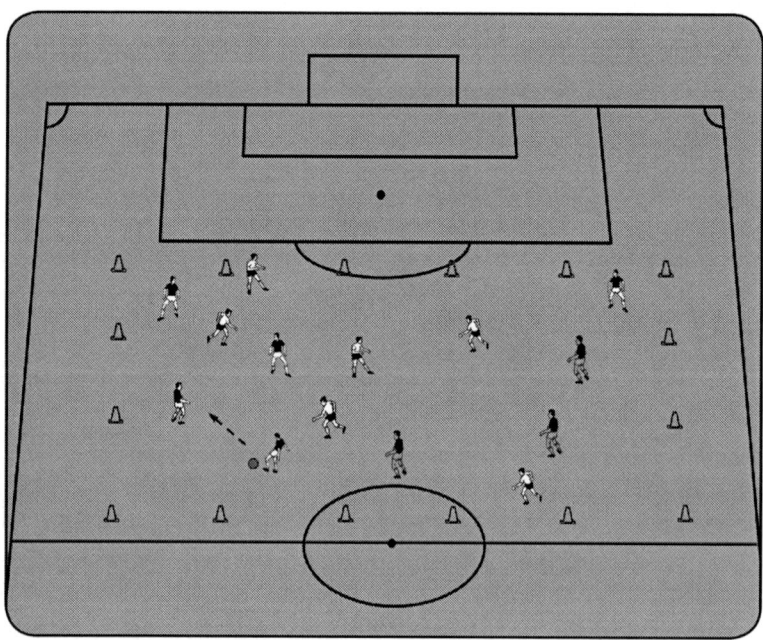

8 v 8 Keep-Away To Targets

Using the same field dimensions as the previous exercise, the teams are now evenly numbered (8 v 8). Each team has a target player in the end zone. Upon change of possession, the players switch the target player. The focus of the session is to play quick one or two-touch combination play to the middle players before playing a ball out to a wide player who serves a long ball in the air to the target player.

Upon receiving the ball, the target player passes back out to the feet of a teammate, who then turns and plays to the opposite zone before attempting to return play back to target player. The pace of the play increases with more intense defensive pressure.

8 v 8 Half Field With Keepers

The game progresses to a half field 8 v 8 game with keepers in each goal. The tempo is now game speed with hard aggressive defense and tackles. The game continues with fast combination play through the middle whenever possible.

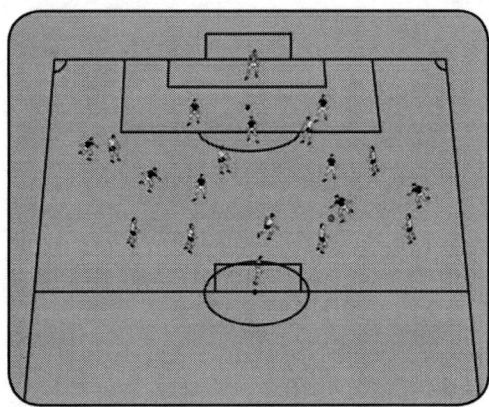

These sessions were conducted by Bob Warming, head men's coach at Creighton University. They were conducted at the WORLD CLASS COACHING International Coaching Seminar in December 2004 in Omaha, Nebraska. The sessions are a selection of Bob's favorite small-sided games.

4 v 4 + 2 Neutrals

On a 40 x 20-yard field, two teams of four play against each other, with two neutral players inside the field as all time attackers and two player at each end as target players. A point is awarded for every pass played into a target player on the end line. When you score at one end, you then attack the other.

Coaching Points

• Two neutral players hunt the ball - but not together
• Narrow field dimensions - think about playing up, back and through
• Body position should be side-on to the player with the ball
• Look before you receive the ball - have a target picked out first
• Look for splits of the defenders with first touch
• Bend your run when coming to support neutral player on end line

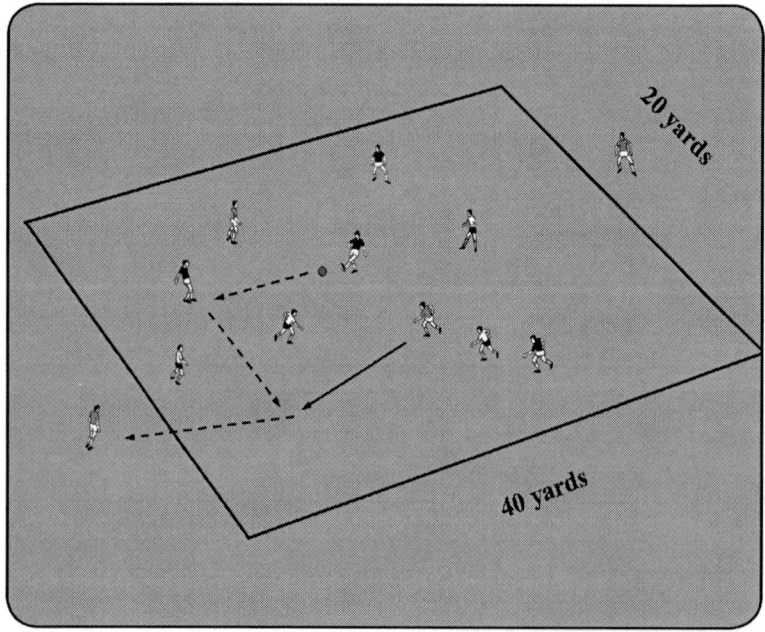

Progressions

· Rotate the field dimensions, making the field wider than it is long
· Play 4 v 4 + 2 to full sized goals and end players move to side line. Two neutral players play as all time attackers in the middle but are restricted to two touch only. Outside supporting players play one touch only

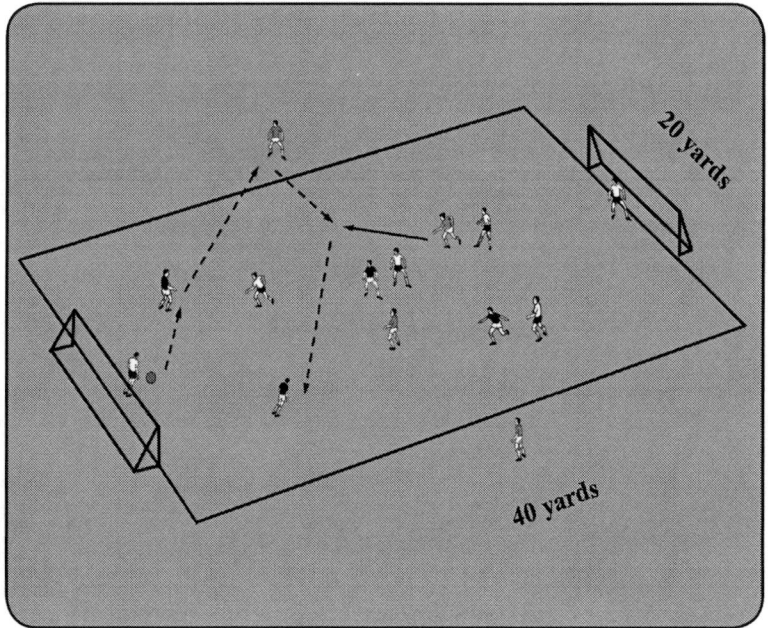

These games are part of sessions that were observed by Daryn "Ozzie" White, Director of Coaching for Ankeny S.C. in Iowa, along with Sean Kehoe. Wimbledon F.C. , then in the English First Division, became the first club in British soccer to re-locate their franchise from South London to Milton Keynes. Under the guidance of manager Stuart Myrdoch, 1st team coach Jimmy Gilligan, Academy Director Martin Heather and Under 19's coach, Gary Smith, the following sessions were samples of the daily routine of some of the teams within the club.

5 v 5 + Targets

In a 40 x 40-yard area, players play 5 v 5 + 1 with two target players placed on each side of the area. Target players only have one touch while the remaining players use two.

Coaching Points

• Pace of pass
• Stretch area, make the space as big as possible
• Play the ball forward quickly: penetrate
• Body shape
• As the ball travels, support players should fix angles and distances
• Think two or three moves ahead

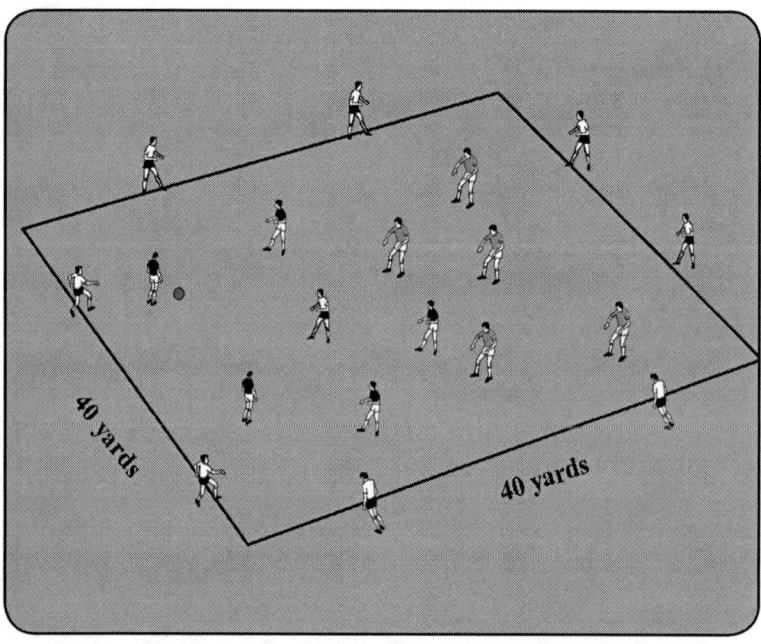

5 v 5 + 1 with Target's

Using a 40 x 30-yard area, players play 5 v 5 + 1 to two small goals. Target players are now placed in each corner of the field and are allowed to move between cones, changing angles for receiving and returning passes.

Rules and Restrictions

The neutral player is restricted to one, two or unlimited touches. The target players are restricted to one touch. The 10 other players play two-touch. If a goal is scored in open play, one point is awarded, if a team scores after using a target player, three points are awarded.

Coaching Points

- Play forward quickly
- Penetrate early
- Support the ball as it travels
- Decision making

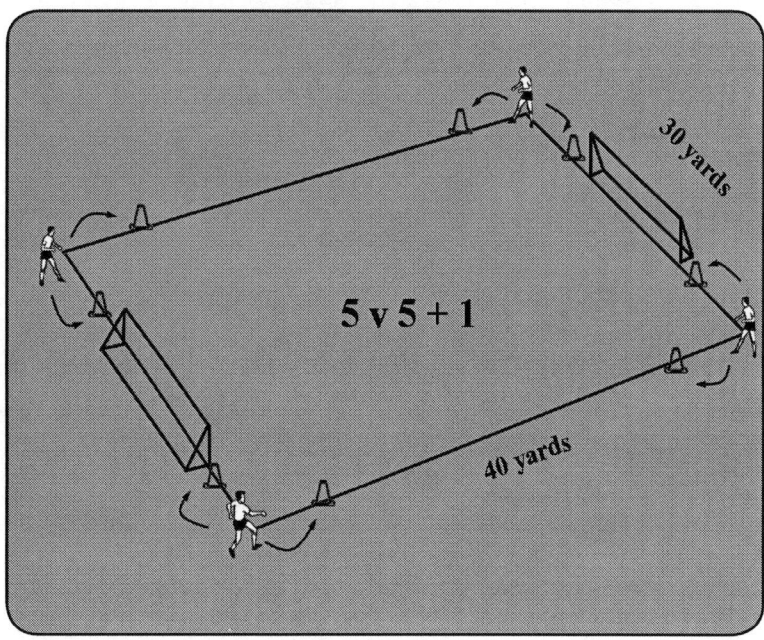

Group Two
Play a 4 v 4 small-sided game with target players placed at each end of the area.

Rules
- Five connecting passes equals one point (one to two-touch restriction)
- Play a pass to a target player in-between the coned goals, following a give-and-go combination

Progression
- Keep possession and change direction after scoring
- Find the target player with an aerial pass

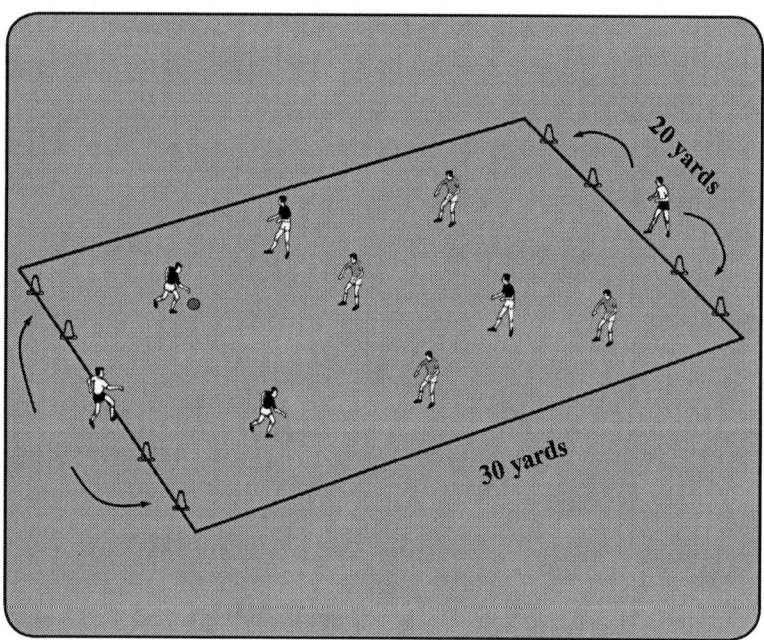

The following series of small-sided games focusing on overlaps are presented by Wayne Harrison Director of Player and Coach Development for Eden Prairie Soccer Club in Minnesota. Harrison is also the author of a number of best-selling coaching books. This is Part One of a two part series.

This is a game situation developing the overlapping theme using simple examples of overlap runs in a 4 v 4 game. For simplicity and to ensure overlaps are practiced, from throw-ins or goal kicks, set the condition that the opposition can't move until a non-competitive overlap has been performed. Once this has been done, and the overlapping player has received the ball, the opponents can begin to play.

Every time a player passes the ball forward in the game, they must perform an overlap move with the receiver. This shows a pass and overlap run from (3) working with receiver (4) who brings the ball inside to create more space outside for the run of (3).

If successfully performed in a wide area (where most overlaps will occur), then in this example, (2) is now making a run into space to receive the cross.

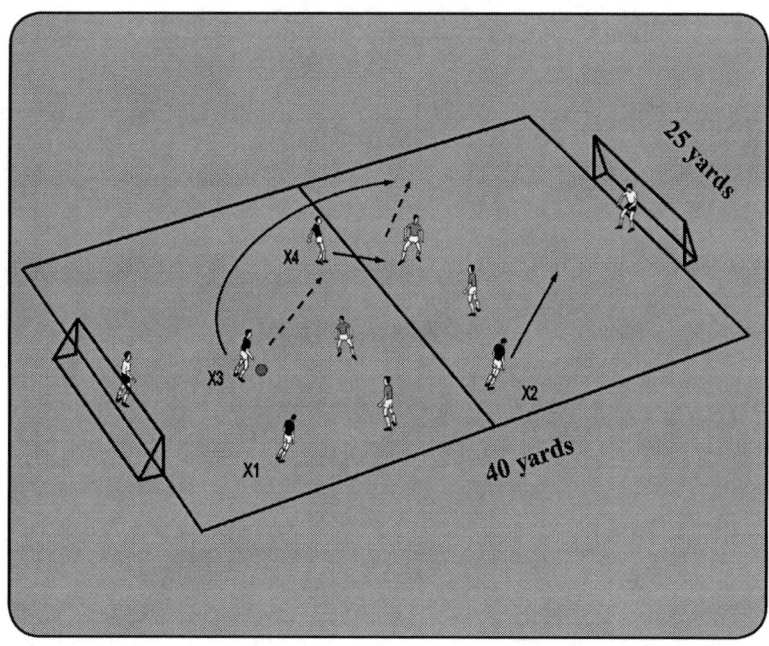

Taking the overlapping game into a 6 v 6 situation, which is pertinent to U9's, we have an example of a back player (3) working with a midfield player (4), performing an overlap in a wide area of the field.

(4) brings the ball inside to clear the space for (3), who is making the overlapping run, note also: striker (6) moving inside to clear the space in front of (3) taking the defender (A) away also. (3) can now continue the run forward with the ball into space to get into a likely crossing position.

If (A) were to stay in the space to try to stop the forward run of (3), then (6) is available to receive a pass inside from (3).

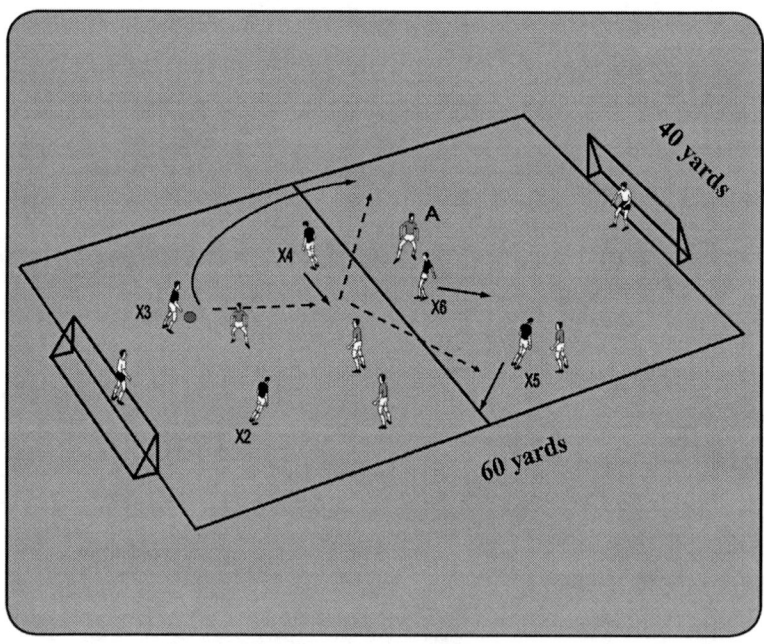

Now take it into an 8 v 8 game, the set-up pertinent for U10's.

Here is an example of a throw-in situation where the uncontested overlap to begin the game is shown.

You could argue this is an "under-lap" because it is coming inside, but it is still technically passing and overlapping the receiver.

Of course the "when" and "where" of overlapping is important, and this must be emphasized and taught, but we just want to get the players performing overlap movements to begin with.

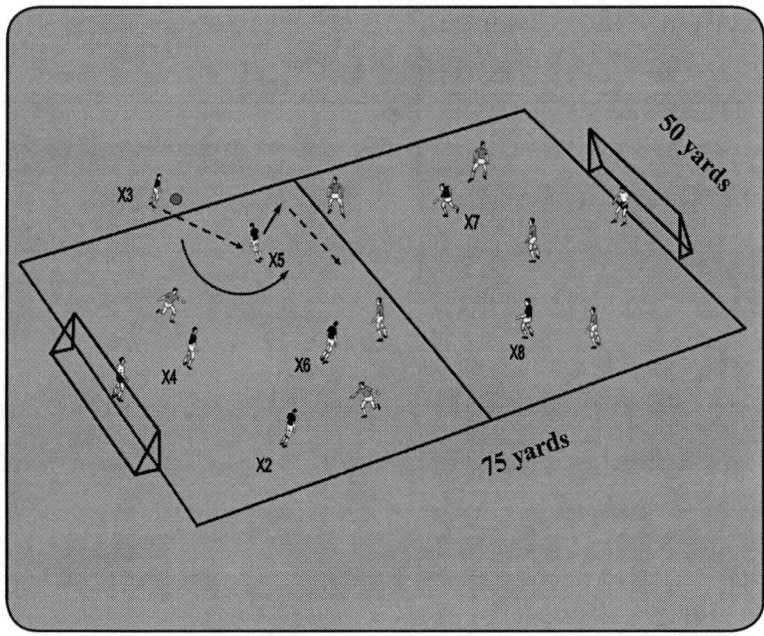

The following are exercises undertaken at the Celtic Youth Academy with various age groups from U12 - U19. The drills were conducted by then Academy Director, Tommy Burns and Academy coaches Danny McGrain and Willie McStay. Burns went on to become the coach of the Celtic First Team.

3 v 3 + Target Player

Teams play 3 v 3 in a 20 x 20-yard grid. Each team has a target player in an "end zone" at each end of the grid. Teams play keep-away for eight three-minute games.

Coaching Points

- Keep ball
- Change direction
- Unbalance defense
- Only use target players when needed
- Target players receive, then drive into the grid and commit defenders (target player rotates with passer from the grid)

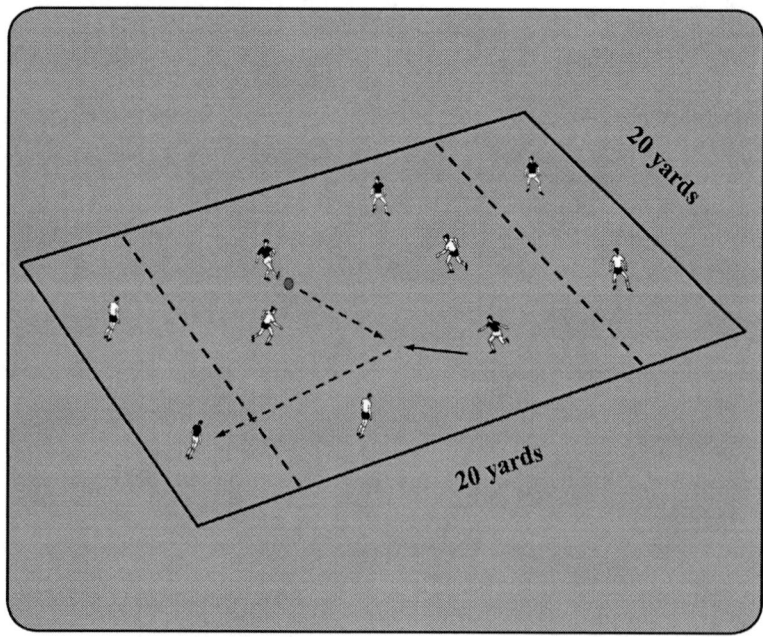

4 + 1 v 3

Four attacking players on each side of a 15 x 15-yard grid, with another attacking player in the center. Three defenders pressure ball from inside of the grid. Attackers pass ball around and try to hit central teammate.

Coaching Points
- Body shape
- Disguise
- Decision making
- Pass selection
- Target players
  - Open up
  - One-touch
  - Body shape
  - Disguise
  - Awareness

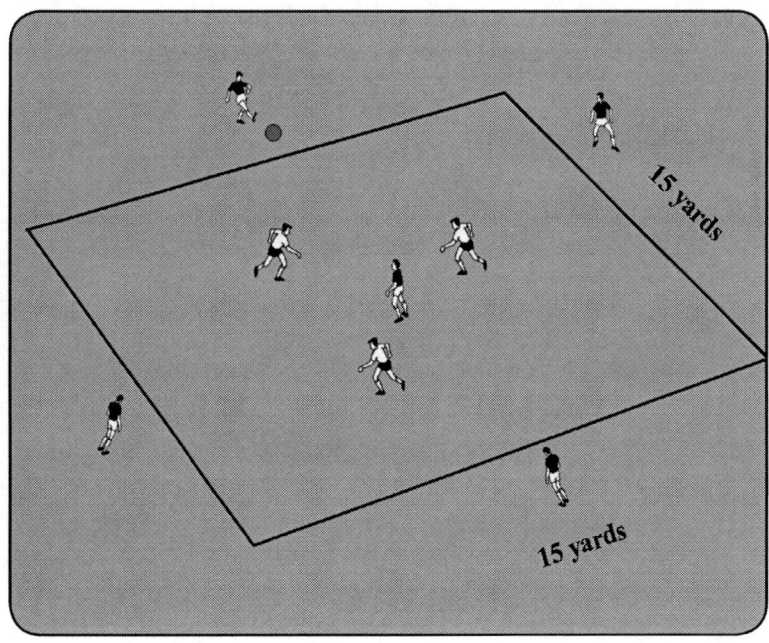

This game was a part of a session that was observed during pre-season training in Florida, February 2000. This was a morning training session conducted at the time they were practicing twice a day.

Six Goal Game

Play 10 v 10 on a 50 x 60-yard field with one neutral player that plays for the team in possession. Each team defends three small goals. Have spare balls around the field to keep play moving. If the ball goes out-of-bounds it is put back in play with a kick-in. Play for 20 minutes.

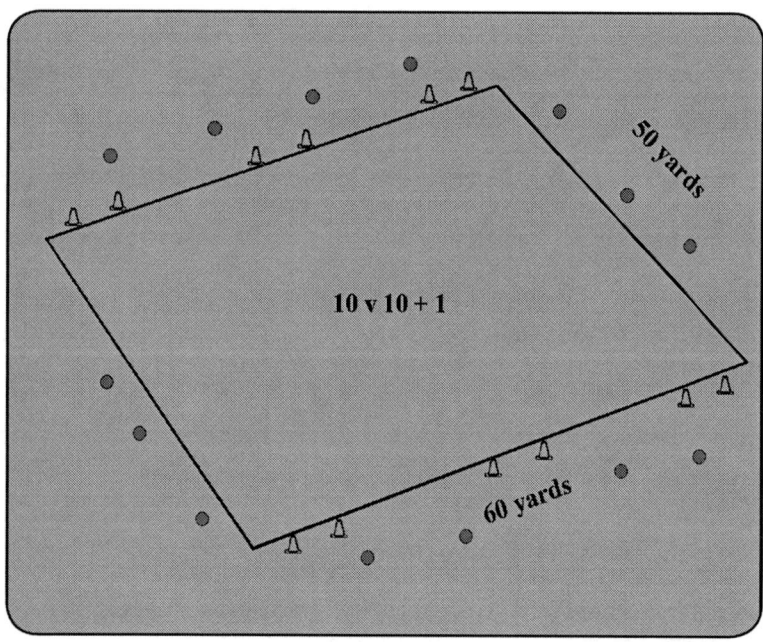

This game was part of a session contributed by long-time subscriber Gerry Canavan. The session was conducted by Dave Bassett of Barnsley F.C.

3 v 3 v 3 Keep-Away

Organize three teams of three players in a 25 x 25-yard area. Each team has a different colored jersey. Two teams combine to play 6 v 3 keep-away against the other three players. The team that is responsible for losing possession becomes the defending team. Play for 25 minutes starting with three-touch, progressing to two-touch and then one-touch. Have a supply of balls around the perimeter to keep the game flowing.

Coaching Points
- Body shape should change in relation to the ball's movement.
- Good passing and receiving technique
- Work hard - chase to get the ball back

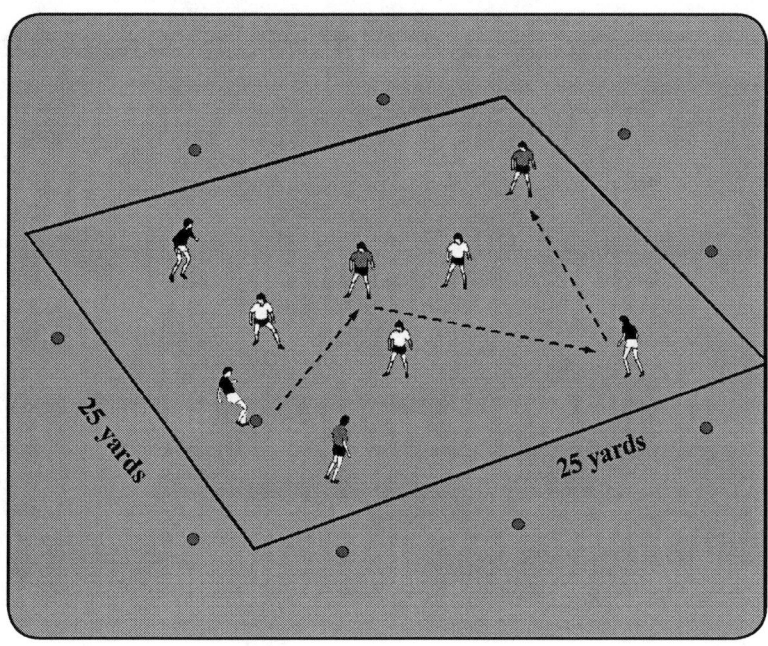

This game was part of a session that was contributed by Warren Joyce, then Leeds United U17 youth team coach. The practices is a technical/tactical session that can be used as a warm-up focusing on passing, receiving and movement.

Progression To Small-Sided Game

The objective of the session is to work specifically on passing, receiving, movement off the ball, communication and finishing. The field is set up as shown in diagram 92 in a 40 x 35-yard area with four small goals or flags - two placed at the ends and two on the sides. The players are split into two teams of six. There are no goalkeepers and the team that scores a goal maintains possession.

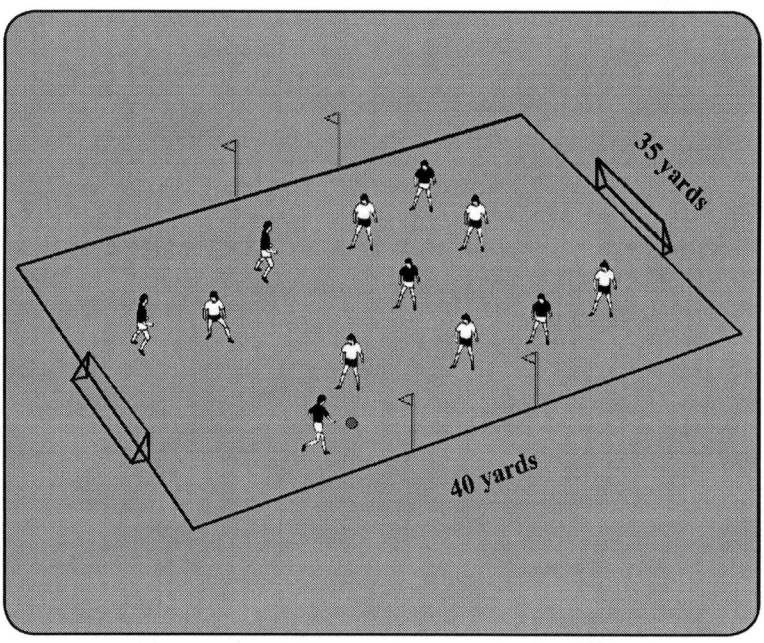

Game One

Play 6 v 6. Following six passes, the team in possession may score in any of the four goals.

Progressions

- Score in any one of the four goals with no conditions
- Hit the back of the net without the ball bouncing
- Can only score with a one-touch finish

Game Two

The game is limited in time to three minutes. One team (dark team) is given possession and their task is to maintain possession for the three minutes. Should the other team gain possession, then they are limited to two-touch and four passes before they can score, with a one-touch finish, in any of the four goals. Following every goal, the dark team regains possession.

Repeat the game with the white team having possession and the dark team trying to score as many goals as possible within the three minutes. The team that scores the most goals in the three minutes wins.

Coaching Points

- The best way to stop the other team from scoring is to keep the ball for as long as possible within the three minutes.
- First touch, passing ability and movement off the ball are crucial to the success of keeping possession
- Encourage good habits of communication

General Coaching Points For Game One and Two

- Passing awareness - encourage the players to 'have something in mind' before they receive the ball
- Encourage as many 'give-and-go's' as possible in order to achieve a better position to pass again or to shoot
- Man-for-man Marking - highlight staying with the runners and to 'switch on' as soon as possession is lost
- Communication - highlight the importance of good communication in terms of who matches up with who

Depending on your theme and focus, you can get several sessions from this basic organization.

This game is from a session conducted by David Williams, fromer youth team coach at Manchester United.

Warm-Up
After a 10-minute jog and stretch, the players quickly got organized into pairs and started passing and moving over a half-field. The players were about 15 yards apart from each other.

Progressions
- The player with the ball dribbles, the player without the ball moves one direction then checks back to receive the pass
- The player without the ball moves away from his partner then quickly turns and checks back to receive the pass
- Add imagination and variation to the passes
- Move to 30 yards apart
- Increase the speed of play

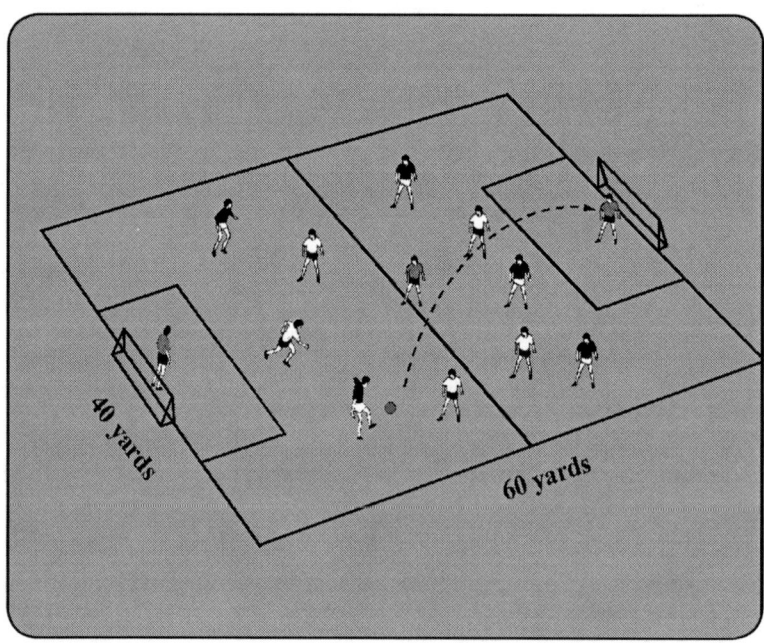

Coaching Point

The receiver has the option of where and when he will move and check back for the ball. Therefore, the player in possession should look up and read the movements of his partner.

Possession

On a marked-out field 60 x 40 yards, play 5 v 5 + 1 with goalkeepers. Each team can score at either end. The goals are not used. A goal can only be scored by a lofted pass from the opposite half of the field and into the goalkeeper's hands without touching the ground. After a goal, the goalkeeper distributes the ball to the scoring team. For example, in diagram 5, the player in possession has just scored by passing a high ball to the goalkeeper's hands. The goalkeeper would then keep the game going by passing the ball back to a player on the dark team. The team in possession can use the goalkeepers to pass back to in order to keep possession. The first 15 minutes were played with a three-touch restriction. The last 10 minutes were played two-touch.

Coaching Points

- Defensively - mark players
- Defensively - close and pressure to stop the long scoring pass
- Offensively - use the warm-up movements to lose your marker
- Goalkeepers - use feet to control the ball if it hits the ground before it reaches you

Observations

- I saw David Williams do a similar variation of this small-sided game last year. David told me he has many variations of the game that can be used to get across many different coaching points.
- It is a great game to involve the goalkeepers - they get to practice high balls, back-passes, and distribution with both hands and feet.
- The game was played at a quick pace with many one-touch passes.
- Many of the goals that were scored with a one-touch pass were set up by a teammate 'stunning' the ball.
- The players were always aware of their defensive responsibilities.

This game is part of a session contributed by Mike Matkovic the director of coaching for the Chicago Magic Soccer Club. Mike is a U.S.S.F. National Staff Coach, holds a USSF 'A' License.

Four Goal Game

Play from penalty area to penalty area with cones marking two small goals at both sides of the penalty areas. Play 8 v 8 plus two neutral players that play for the team in possession. Usually the two neutral players are our goalkeepers and they are allowed to use their hands. Shape the team in a 3-3-2 formation and have offside in effect. Place balls around the field to keep play moving. Play three 5-minute games - unlimited touches, two touch and unlimited touches.

Coaching Points

- Defensively - stay compact, when to press and when drop off
- Offensively - switch the point of attack, quick play, when to play around v when to get behind
- Transition - where to play the first pass

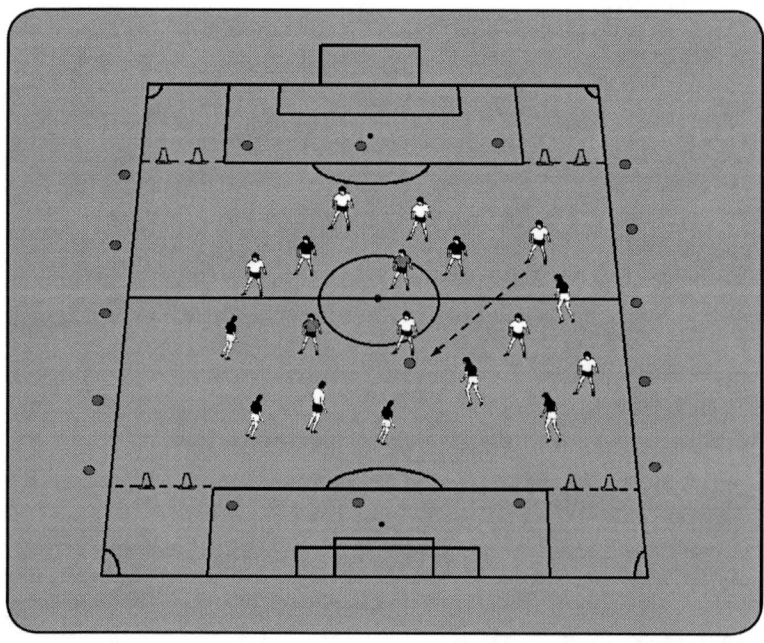

These games are from a U11 training session conducted at the Crystal Palace Youth Academy.

2 v 1 End Zone Game

Mark a 20 x 10-yard area plus 5-yard end zones. In the 20 x 10-yard grid, play two darks v one white. In the end zones, have one dark player and two white players. The objective is for the two dark players inside the grid to pass to their teammate in either end zone who controls and then passes back. Change players every few minutes.

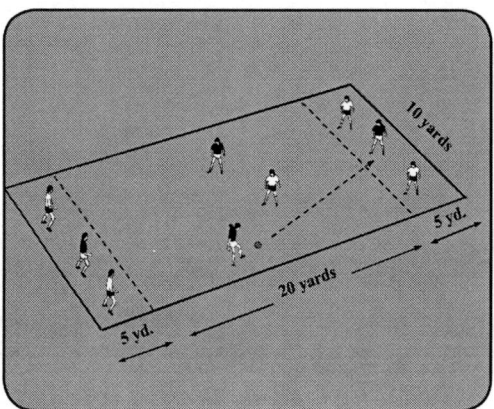

Progression

Play 3 v 2 inside the grid with one white player and one dark player in each end zone. Again, the objective is to pass the ball to a teammate in the end zone. This time however, when his teammate receives the ball, his objective is to attempt to turn and take the ball over the end-line of the end zone under control while being defended by the white player in the end zone. If the defender blocks the turn he can pass back inside the grid and play continues.

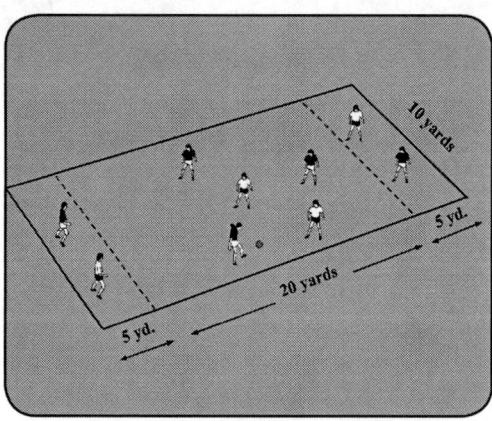

Small-Sided Possession Game
The players then play 5 v 5 keep-away in a 40 x 30-yard grid. Five consecutive passes score a point.

Four Goal Game
Play 5 v 5 in a 25 x 25-yard grid with four small goals as shown below, with each team defending two goals.

Practice ended with both teams combining to play a 9 v 9 scrimmage on a half-field for the last 30 minutes.

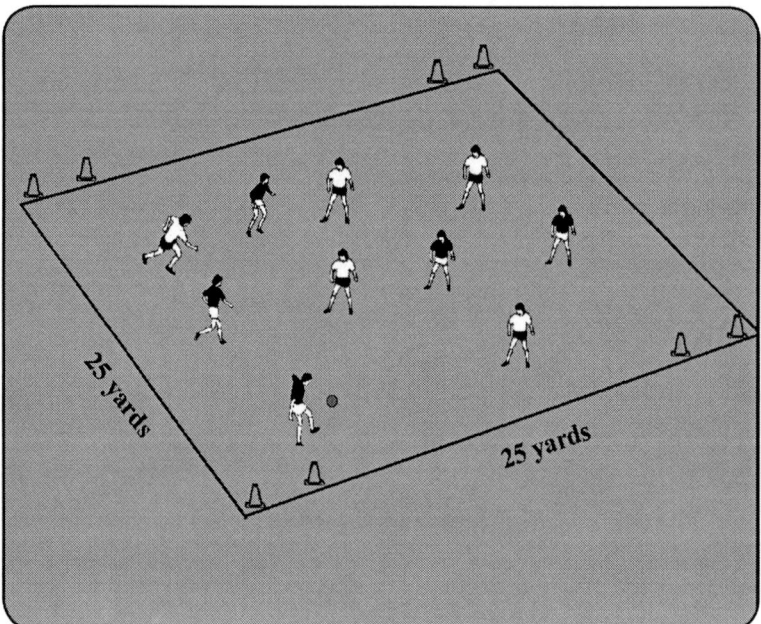

This small-sided game is part of a session conducted by Bob Gansler, formerly of the K.C. Wizards. it's aimed at developing a good first touch for youth players. The session was part of the KSYSA workshop and was conducted with the Kansas 86 Boys ODP team.

Two v Two v Two Keep-Away

Organize three pairs of players in different colored jerseys. The dark and gray players combine to play keep-away from the white players. The team responsible for losing possession alternates with the white players and become defenders.

Coaching Points

- Quick transition
- Use the inside and outside of the foot to control the ball and keep it moving - using the sole of the foot slows the ball movement
- Look for the penetrating pass that splits the defenders - it is usually a one-touch pass
- Get your body in position when receiving the ball so you can see all your options
- Kicking the ball out-of-bounds is not enough for the defenders to change places - they must win the ball

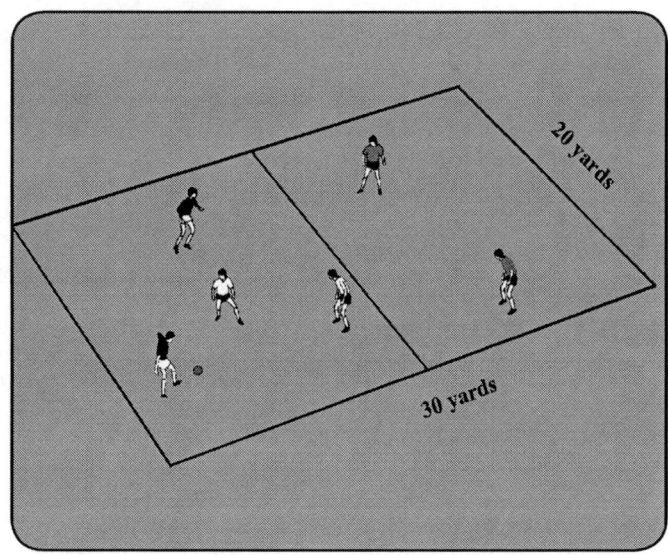

Small-Sided Game
Play 4 v 4 with each team defending two small goals as shown in diagram 30.

Variations
• The defending team has one player kneeling
• The attacking team has one player kneeling

Coaching Points
• Play two touch or three touch
• Look for the penetrating pass

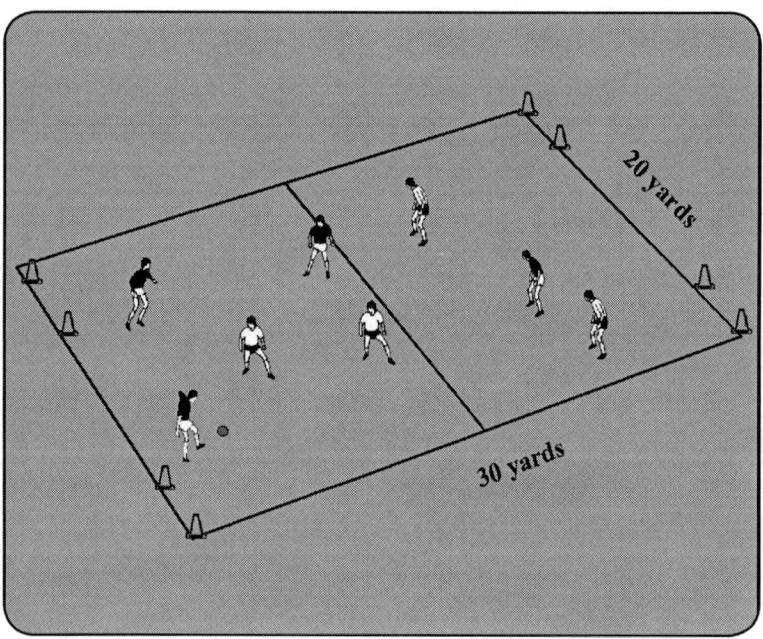

This session was contributed by Jeff Pill, then U.S. Women's National Staff Coach, U.S. Women's U18 National Team Assistant Coach and U14 Region One Director of Coaching. The small-sided games from these practices are part of the curriculum of the Region One U14 Girls ODP camp. You can find more of Jeff's training sessions at www.eteamz.com/soccer/pills/jpill.htm

4 v 4 v 4 Middle Zone Game

Organize three teams of four in a 50 x 30-yard area with a 10-yard middle zone as shown in diagram 53. The dark team has four players in one end zone and the white team has four players in the other end zone. The objective is for the dark and white teams to keep the ball away from the grey team. This can be done by passing to their own players or passing long into the other end zone. The grey team can send only two players into an end zone at one time. The two other grey players must remain in the middle zone. The grey team can get out of the middle by replacing the team that loses the ball out-of-bounds or by stealing it from one team and passing to the other team in the opposite end zone.

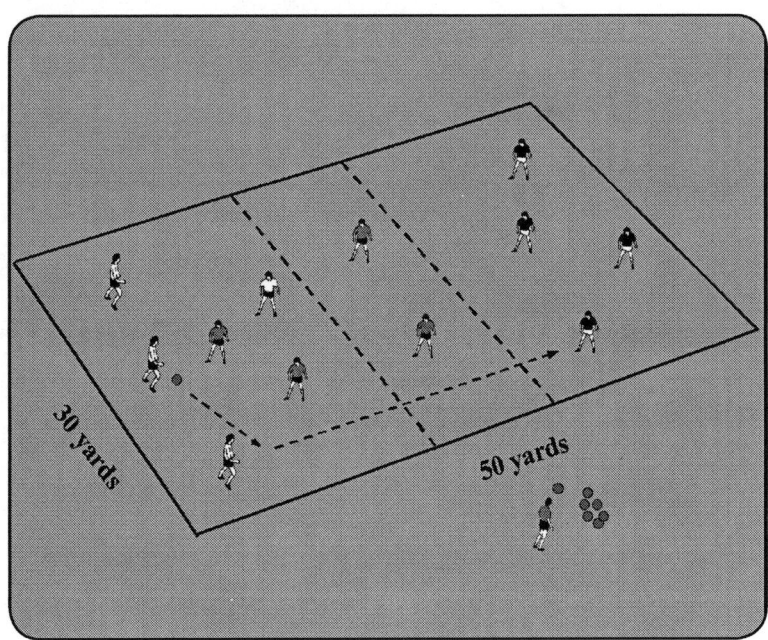

End Zone Game

Play 4 v 4 on a 50 x 30-yard field with 5-yard end zones as shown in diagram 54. The objective is for the attacking team to attack one end zone. If the defending team wins the ball, they can attack either end zone. Players are not allowed to defend inside the end zones.

End practice with a conditioned game focusing on correct technique, team shape and possession/penetration decisions.

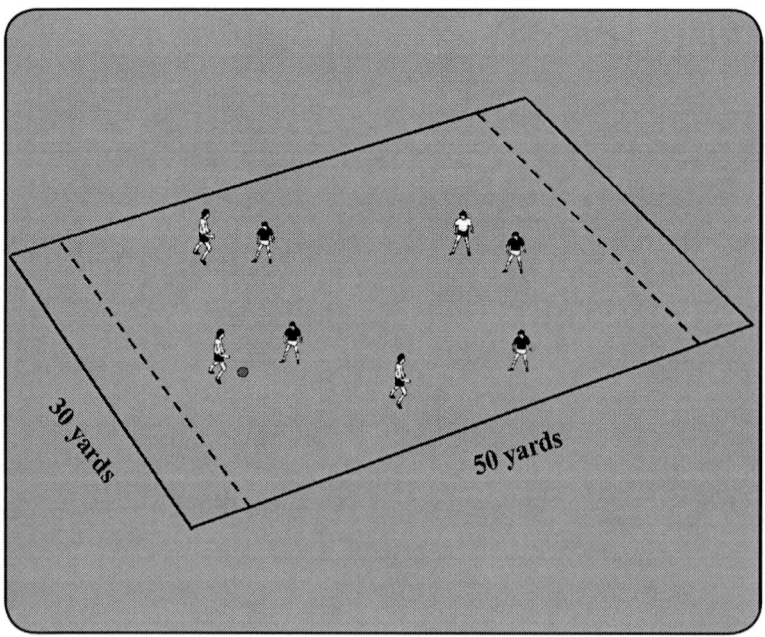

These games are part of re-season training with the Dallas Burn. As observed at Orlando, Florida - Pre-season 2001

Combination Plays

In diagram 86, the groups splits into 4 v 4 situations with two neutral players on the outside of the 30 x 25-yard playing area. The objective of the drill is for the team in possession to get the ball under control and into one of the end zones. If the team is successful, they keep the ball and attack the opposite end zone.

Conditions
- The outside players use one touch only
- Inside players are restricted to two touches
- To score, the players must receive the ball before entering the end zone

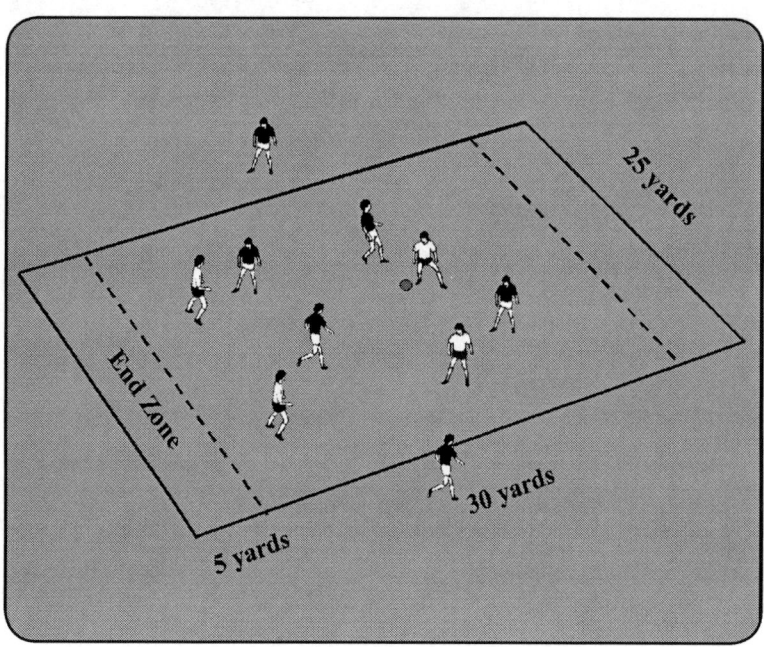

Progression One

Using the same area, the neutral players move to the end zones and act as target players. To score, the team in possession must receive the ball back from one of the neutral players. Following a goal, the team can then attack the opposite end zone.

Coaching Points

- Two-touch inside the area and one touch in the end zone
- Neutral players must move continuously to give an angle to receive the ball
- As soon as the target man is hit, the team must get players into position to receive the lay-off in order to score

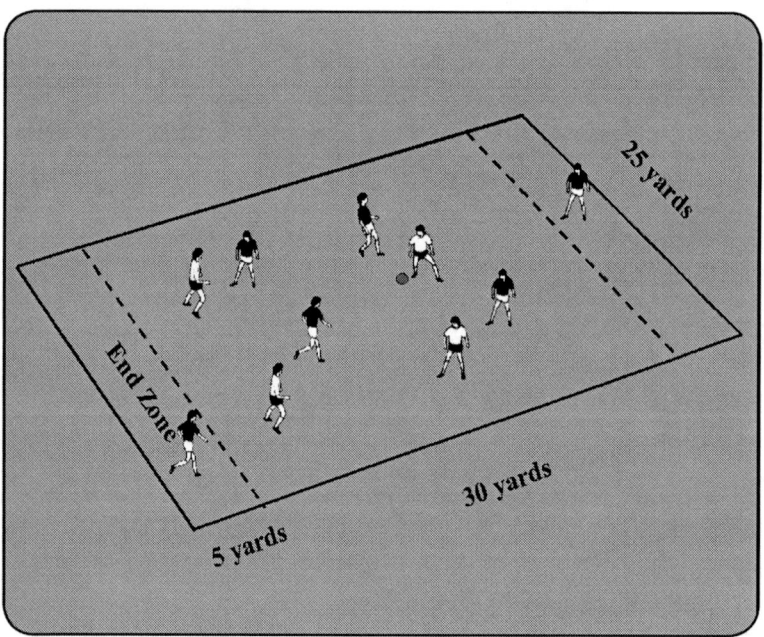

Progression Two
Play 5 v 5 in the same area with teams having to get the ball under control in the end zone. Then once a goal is scored, instant transition to the opposite end zone is required.

Coaching Points
- Shape of the defense
- Defense to re-group following a goal
- The running and the movement off the ball
- The attackers must maintain their speed of play following a goal being scored
- Use and variation of the long and short options

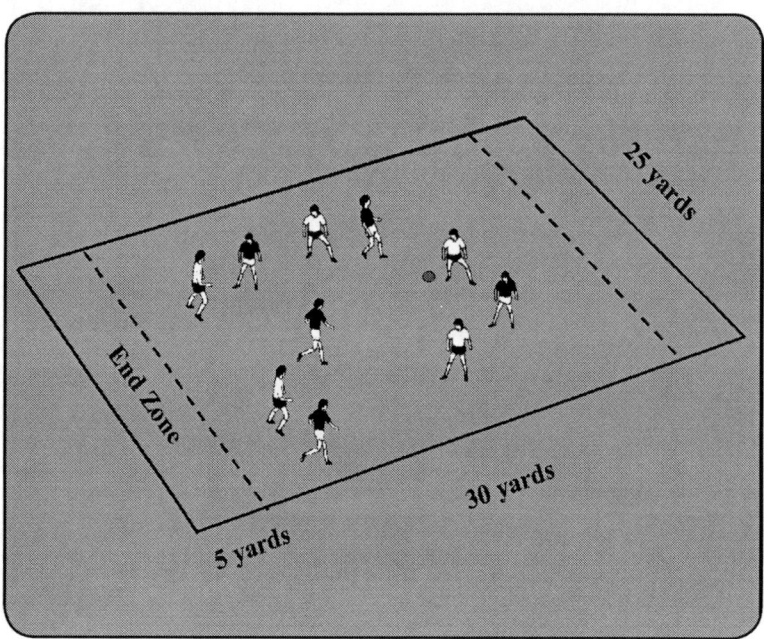

Progression Three

Following another water break, the practice is moved onto a 40 x 30-yard field. Using full-sized goals and goalkeepers, the group played 4 v 4 with neutral players on either side of the field.

Conditions

- The neutral players can only cross or pass the ball, not shoot
- Neutral players again have only one touch
- Unlimited touches allowed inside the field

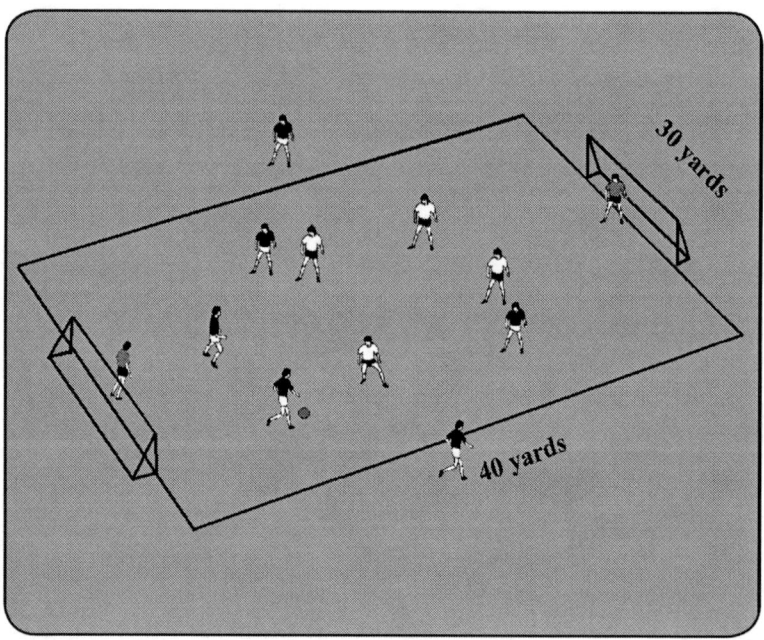

Progression Four

The practice progresses to placing neutral players either side of the goal posts at both ends. The neutral players then act as target players who give lay-off's to the team in possession to shoot and score.

Points

Keep rotating the neutral players who only have one touch

Coaching Points

- Movement off the ball
- Work rate and continuity

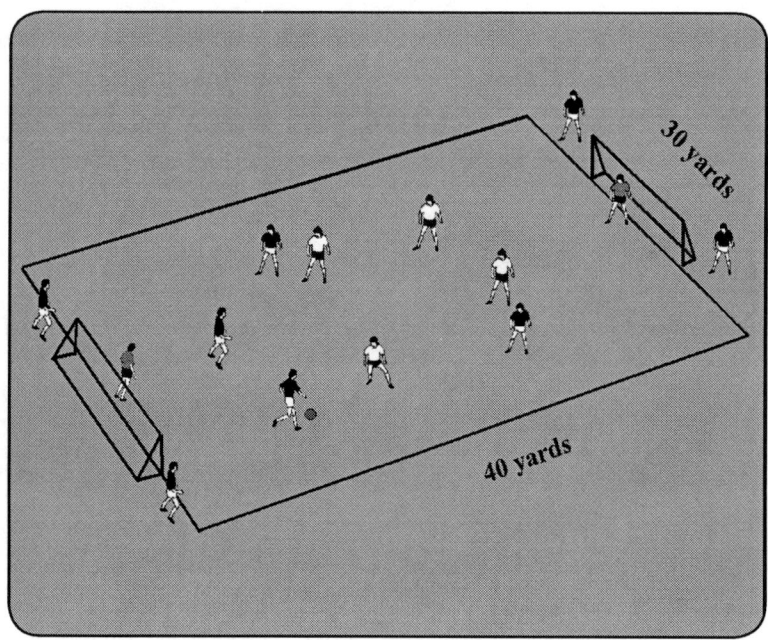

This game was from a session observed during pre-season training in Ft. Lauderdale, February 2000.

Small-Sided Game

Group one then played 7 v 7 plus one neutral player on a 40 x 30-yard field with each team defending two small goals. Play four 5-minute games.

Observations

Head Coach Bob Bradley and assistant Frank Klopas played in the game and were instrumental in motivating the players throughout. I have observed a number of Bradley's practices and he has a knack of wringing every last drop of energy from his players. This game was no exception. With the teams tied in games won and goals scored, Bradley called for the outcome to be decided by a Golden Goal which got the players giving a 110% for the last few minutes before the winners were eventually decided.

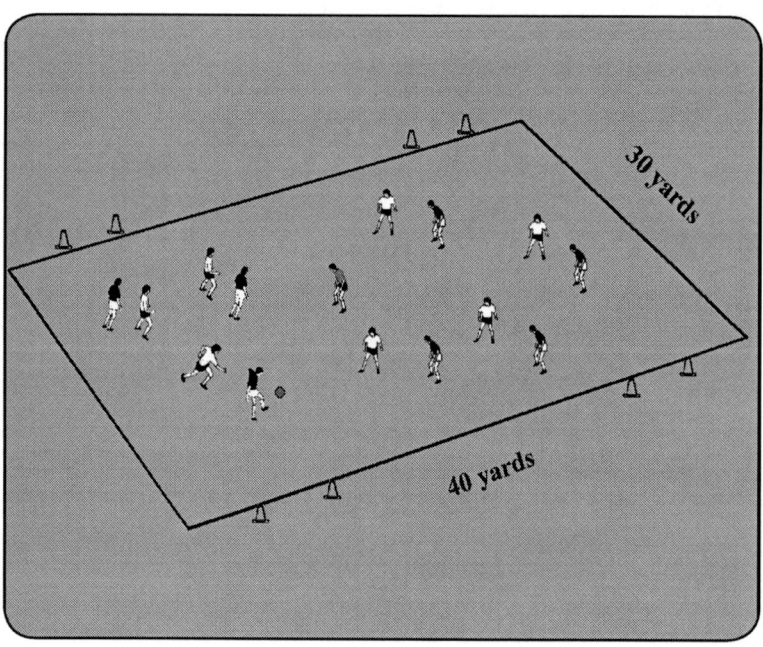

Chapter Three

Shooting and Finishing

This game was from a session observed during pre-season training in Ft.
Lauderdale, February 2000.

Small-Sided Shooting Game

Both groups combine for the final game. Mark a field the size of two penalty
areas with full size goals and goalkeepers. The players are organized into
two teams of 10 and each team of 10 is split into two teams of five. Play 5 v 5
inside with each team having their other five teammates on the perimeter of
the attacking half as shown. The players inside have unlimited touches. The
perimeter players on the side have two touches and the players behind the
goal have one touch. When a goal is scored, the team that concedes the goal
alternates positions with their teammates on the perimeter.

Play for 15 minutes followed by 15 minutes of light jogging and stretching to
cool down.

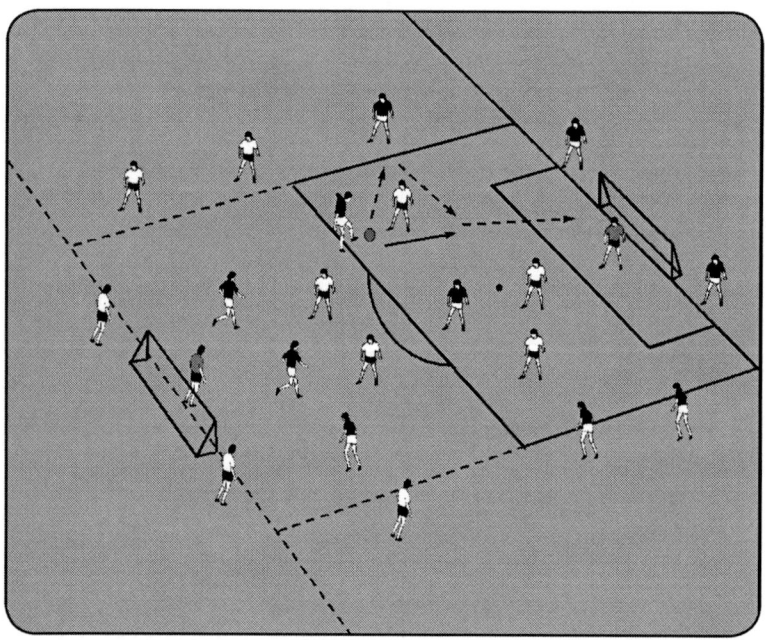

This game was part of a session observed at the Coaches' Super Clinic conducted by Reedswain in New Jersey. Conducted by Lauren Gregg, then assistant coach for the U.S. Women's National Team that won the 1999 World Cup, the session was done indoors in a 40 x 20-yard area. When practicing outdoors, a larger area would be used.

Small-Sided Game

This small-sided game is usually played in an area the size of two 18-yard penalty areas. Organize two teams of three players plus goalkeepers. Position four neutral players at the sides of the goals. Play 3 v 3. The player in possession can pass to a perimeter player who passes back into play with one touch to the passer or one of his teammates as shown in the diagram.

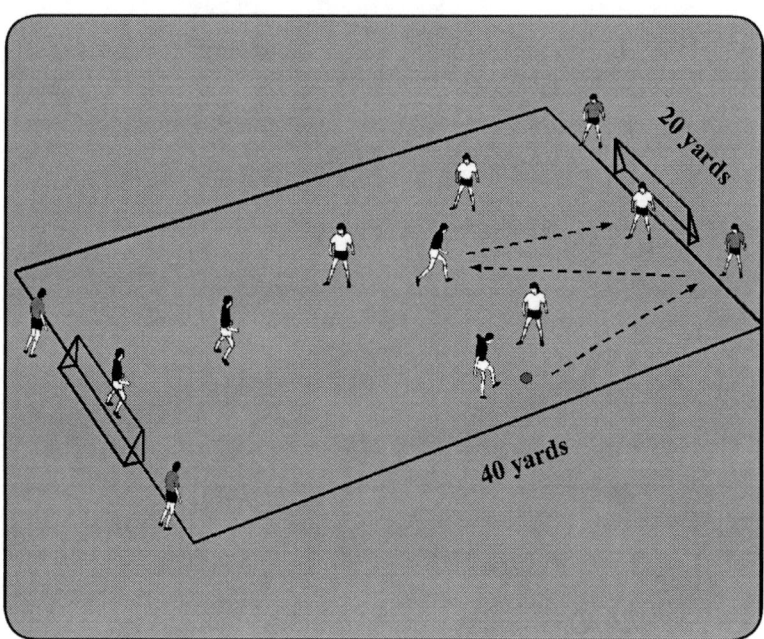

This game is from an article that was contributed by Miles Glynn, assistant DOC for Indiana State Youth Soccer and FC Pride coach. He had the unique experience of observing Real Madrid train at the National Federation's Training Center in suburban Madrid. The squad was intact with Zidane, Beckham and Roberto Carlos leading the array of world class stars. Manager Carlos Quiroz led the session.

Final Activity

Play 5 v 5 to goal with the goals on the goal line and just outside the top of the "D". Because the goals are just 25 yards apart, the players enjoy a lively game in which they are always well within shooting range. Beckham and Zidane are on opposing sides and are the natural catalysts in the game, with Zidane again finding impossible angles and working through tight spaces, and Beckham sending scorching shots into the upper 90's, seemingly at will.

The game begins with unlimited touches and ends with a one-touch restriction.

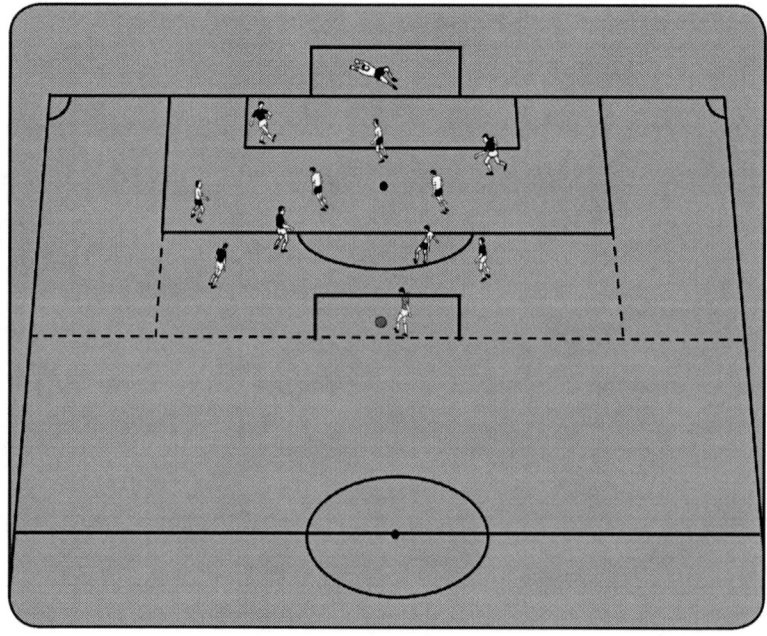

These games are from a session that is part of the youth academy curriculum of Italian Serie "A" club A.C. Perugia and was provided by Bruno Redolfi, Technical Director of A.C Perugia and Antonio Saviano.

3 v 3 and Shoot

Now a 15-yard space is created as a middle section. Within this space a 3 v 3 situation is set up whereby the objective is to cross the opponent's "line" via a pass or by dribbling, and creating a goalscoring situation.

Objectives
- Offensive and defensive collaboration
- Creating space, movement without the ball
- Zone defense

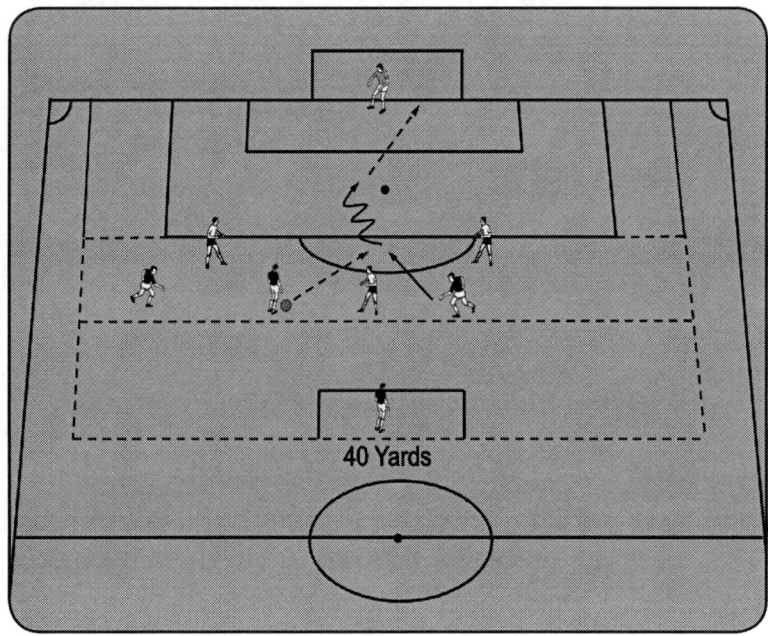

40 Yards

Find The Goal 4 v 4

In a 30 x 20-yard area, two teams try to score in four small goals (which are colored). The team that scores maintains possession of the ball. Teams cannot score in the same goal consecutively.

Variations

The coach indicates in which goal the goal can be scored by lifting the same colored jersey in the air.

Objectives

• Switching play
• Finishing

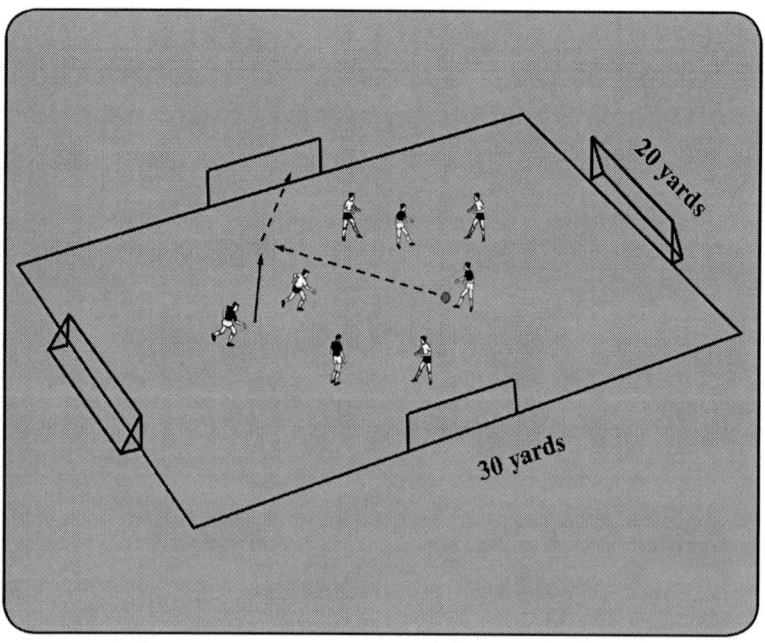

This session was conducted at the Murray Park, Rangers Academy. Both the professional and youth teams train at Murray Park.

This shooting and finishing session was conducted by the coach of the U11 team, Craig Mullholland. The session was conducted indoors on Fieldturf due to heavy rain, making it impossible to train outdoors.

Shooting Game
Each team has four field players and two target players (one on either side of the goal they are attacking). A goal can be scored with or without using the target players.

Progression
The target players are moved to the field for a 7 v 7 scrimmage to end practice.

Coaching Points
The coach didn't stop either game much - when he did, it was almost always to focus on a shooting element.

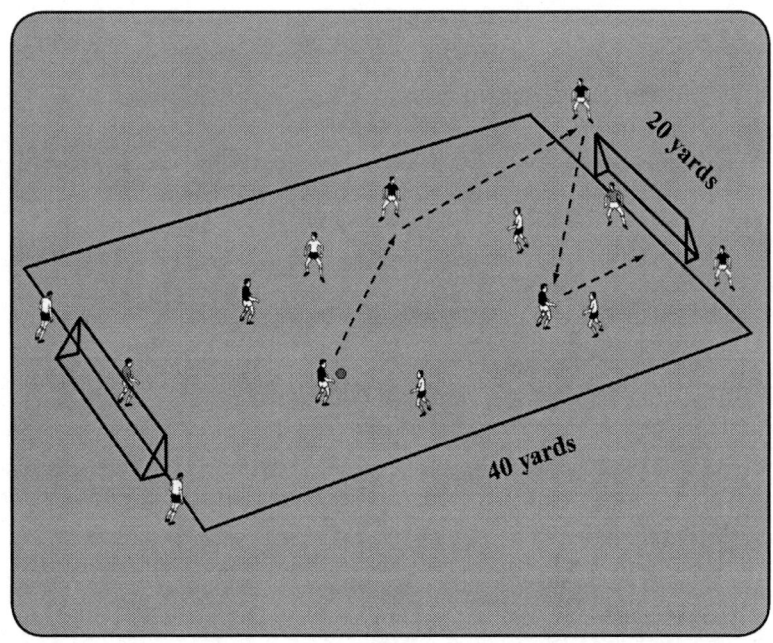

This is a game from a session contributed by Mike Matkovic the director of coaching for the Chicago Magic Soccer Club. Mike is a U.S.S.F. National Staff Coach, holds a USSF 'A' License and is the head coach of the USYSA Region Two '83 team.

Finishing

Place a goal on the edge of the penalty area and extend lines from the 6-yard box as shown in diagram 16. Play 2 v 2 with unlimited touches inside the area. Position players around the perimeter. The perimeter players can move side to side between the cones but are limited to one touch. Play 2-minute games then rotate the teams.

Coaching Points

- Be ready to shoot
- Look for give-and-go's with the perimeter players
- Follow the shots for any rebounds
- Create an attitude to 'finish'
- Do what it takes to score - toe poke, header, etc.

Progression

Allow the perimeter players to shoot.

End practice with a penalty-kick competition followed by a cool down.

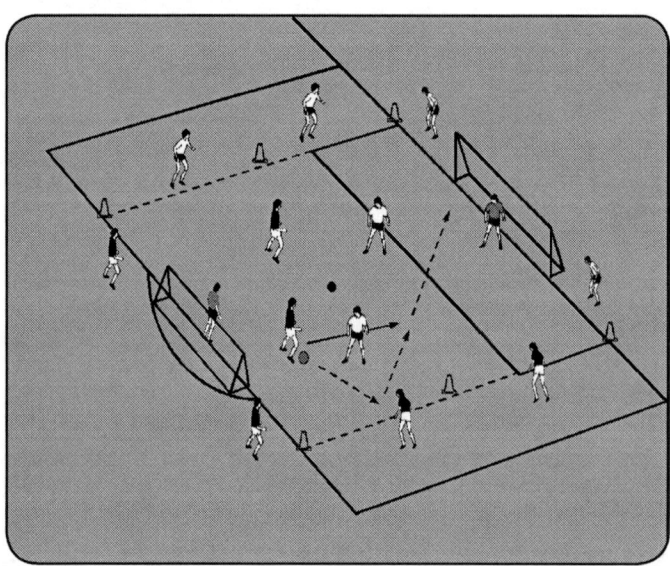

Chapter Four
Crossing & Finishing

This game is part of an article submitted by Paulo Moraes, then Head Coach of Tavares FC, Brazil. Tavares is a Minas Gerais state 3rd division team. Moraes was previously the coach of the U19 team at Guarani BH FC.

Mini-Game
Two teams of four players play with goalkeepers and two additional teammates on the outside of playing area. The field area is one half-field with sidelines running even with the edge of the goal area. Outside players can assist their infield team-mates by passing, crossing or even shooting.

Progression
• Rotate positions

Coaching Points
• Speed of play
• Transition from defense to offense

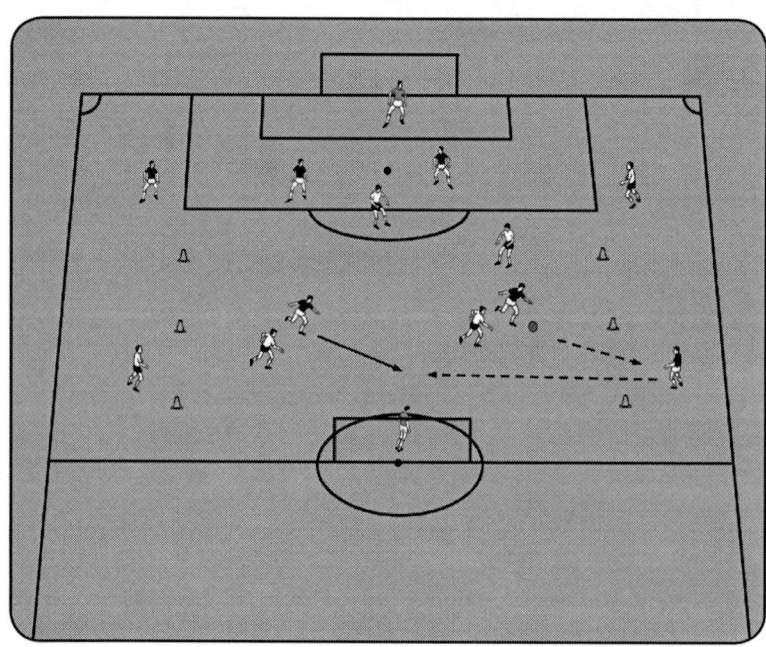

This game is part of a practice conducted by Sammy Lee when he was assistant manager and first team coach at Liverpool F.C. It was observed in October, 2000. Liverpool had just played a game the day before against Derby County in the English Premier League and this practice consisted of the players from the first team squad that hadn't played in that game. This group of players were also due to play a "Friendly" game against a local non-league team that same evening so the practice was rather light.

Throw-Head-Volley

Use full size goals on a 25 x 20-yard area. The ball is passed by throwing it to a teammate who volleys or heads the ball to another teammate or for a shot on goal. Attempt to build up play with passing and moving rather than by throwing long passes.

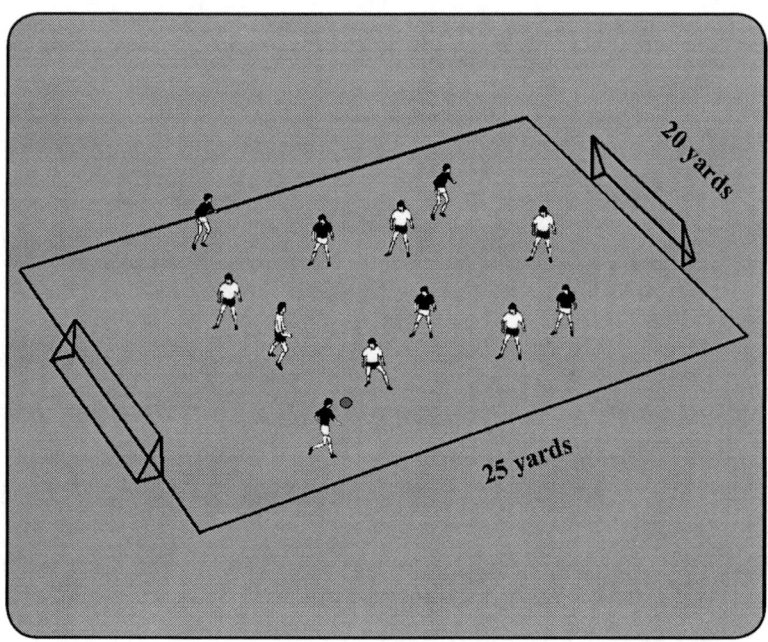

This game is part of an article contributed by subscriber Dave Brown. Brown took part in an overseas coaching tour to the Juventus pre-season training village Sponsored by GoPlay Sports Tours. This is a session from the Juventus team that included all their well known players such as Conte, Davids, Del Pierro, Montero, Nedved, Thuram, Trezeguet and Zambrotta.

Possession Exercises 6 v 6 + 6

Play 6 v 6 keep-away in the marked area with the six remaining "neutral" players on the outside of the field supporting the team in possession. The aim of the game is for the six players to maintain possession before playing to one of the neutral players who then plays a one-touch pass to the perimeter player opposite. The receiving players's successfully controlled long pass equals one point. The neutral team alternates with one of the inside teams on a time basis.

Coaching Point

The level of passing technique, control, speed of defending and concentration required is extremely high for this drill to succeed.

The drill ends with a one-touch 6 v 6 v 6 game.

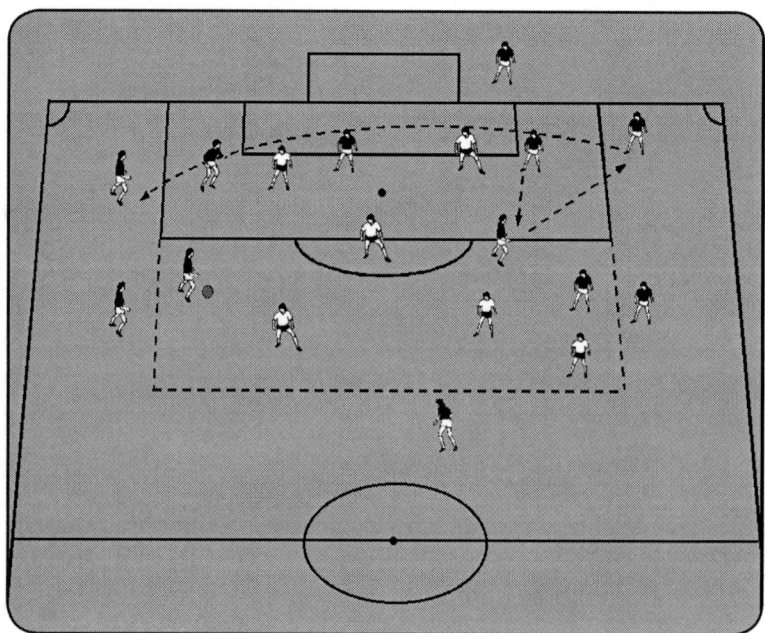

Crossing Game

Play 10 v 10 in one half of the field, with neutral channels on each flank. Any one player at a time can enter the channel to produce a cross (but can not be challenged by a defender). Both teams line up in a 4-3-2 formation. The emphasis of the drill is quality long flighted balls into the attacking zones followed by quality crosses and attacking runs.

The session ends with a no-restrictions scrimmage followed by three cool down laps of the field and some 'indoor' stretching.

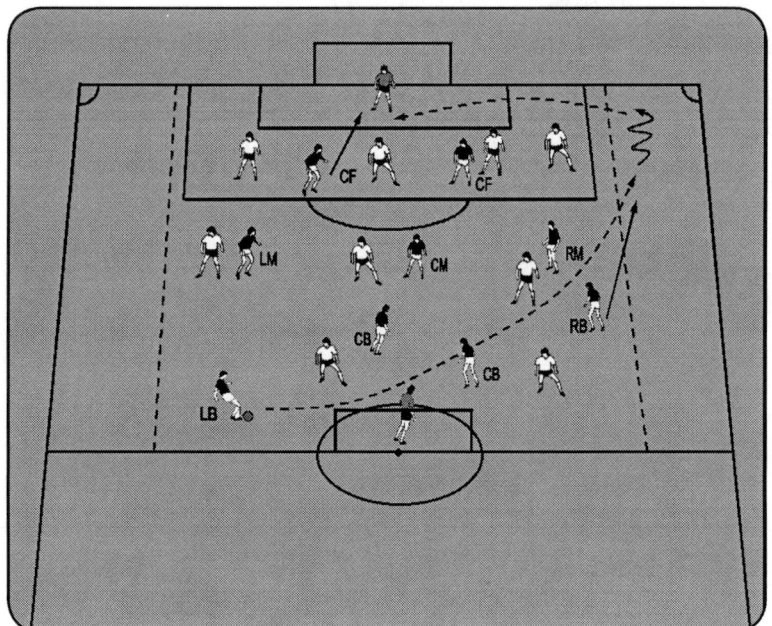

Craig Brown then Manager/Coach of the Scotland National Team and also the Technical Director of the Scottish Football Association provided this game as a part of a complete season. Previously he coached the Scotland U21 team to the U21 World Cup Finals.

Wingers Game

Using half a field, mark a channel down both flanks. Play 3 v 2 in each half. Position four wide players in the channels, two playing in the attacking half for each side. The objective is to play the ball from the back, where the three defenders should have comfortable possession against the two attackers, to a striker who passes wide to the unmarked winger. The cross is delivered to the two strikers, who, at the discretion of the coach, can be supported by one player 'breaking' from the back zone as well as the opposite winger, who, at this point, can come into the central area.

Whenever a goal is scored, or when the move breaks down, the players, or even the goalkeeper, play the ball wide to the unchallenged winger without it first going to one of the front two players. This makes the exercise easier for the less accomplished players.

Much coaching of all aspects of group play is possible, but particular emphasis should be placed on the type of crosses and the movement of the two forwards.

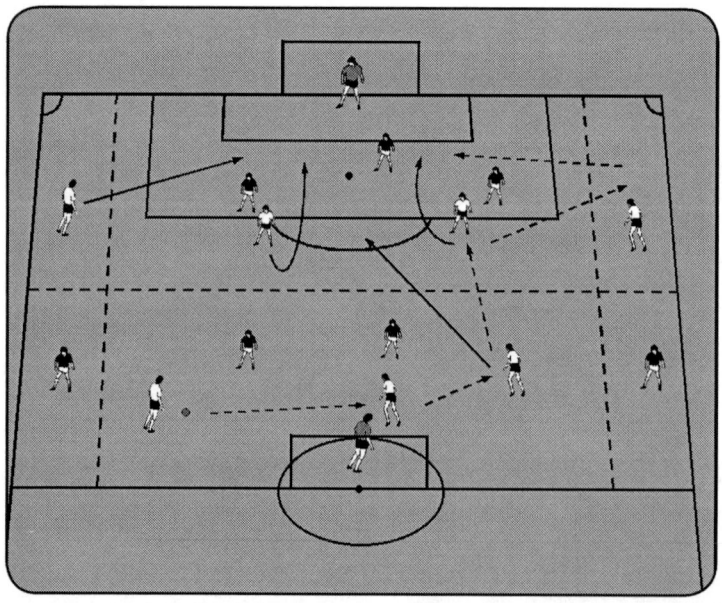

Contributed by Peter Withe then Thailand National Team Coach. Withe had an outstanding playing career, which included a European Cup Championship while at the English Premier League team, Aston Villa. Prior to taking the Thailand National Team position, Withe coached at a number of clubs including Wimbledon and Aston Villa of the English Premier League.

9 v 9 Offside Shooting

I devised this practice to solve the problems I had with players having a tendency to run too early and thus into an offside position to receive a pass, plus to teach players to pass the ball into space rather than to the player.

The practice is 9 v 9 in the middle third of a full field that is marked into thirds with lines also extending from the penalty area as shown in diagram 91. Two coaches are positioned on the lines to see if a player runs into an offside position. The game starts with a coach serving the ball to the dark team who has to make a minimum of three passes before they can pass over the line and into space for a teammate who then goes 1 v 1 against the goalkeeper. Following an attempt at goal, the coach serves a ball to the white team and the game continues.

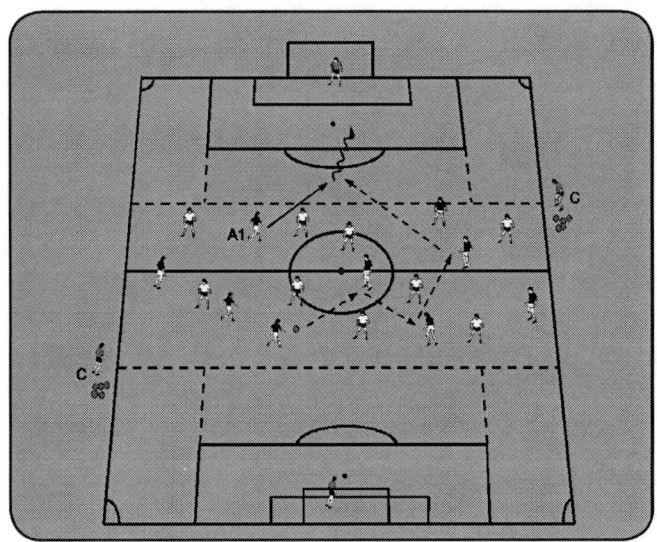

Points Of Observation
The following are the tendencies of the players that this practice will help overcome.
- Rushing the final pass
- Attempting the final pass even when the opportunity is not there
- Play tends to be squeezed in a tight area instead of using the full width of the field
- The final pass is played to the player instead of to space
- The running player (A1) will run too early - offside
- The running player (A1) will run to the wrong area

Coaching Points
- Keep possession until you have a good opportunity to make a quality through-pass into the final third - even if this takes 6, 7 or 8 or more passes
- The timing and weight of the pass is critical - too hard and it will run out-of-bounds - too soft and it could be intercepted
- The timing of the run by A1 should allow him to get to the ball without running offside
- Use the entire area to keep possession and stretch the defending team - this will also open up gaps to make the final pass through

Progression
Introduce a chasing defender (D1) who can chase A1 once he has touched the ball.

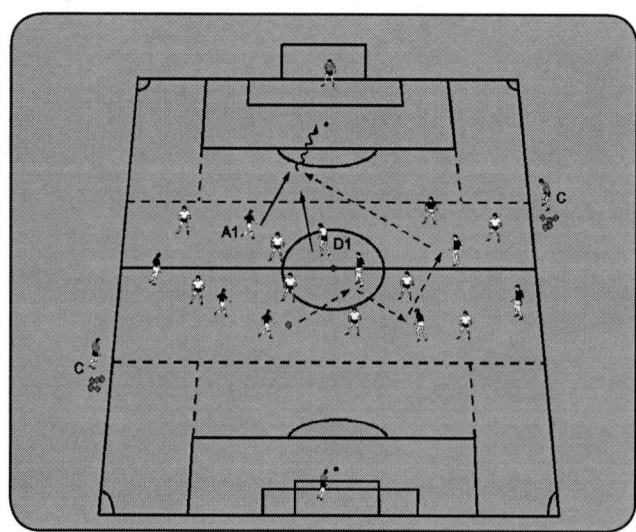

9 v 9 Crossing And Finishing

The same organization as the previous game except this time the final pass is played into the wide area for A3 who attacks the end-line and crosses for two players, A1 and A2 who have made runs into the penalty area.

Coaching Points

- All previous coaching points including timing of runs and weight of passes
- Players A1 and A2 should time their runs so they don't arrive too early
- Players A1 and A2 should stagger their runs as shown, with A1's near post run arriving first and A2's far post run arriving second
- Hit the target with the shot

Variation

The final pass can be made to the opposite flank area to A4 as shown in diagram 94.

A conditioning element can be introduced by asking A1, A2, A3 and A4 to make recovery runs back into the middle third playing area as quickly as possible. To make this effective, the coach should serve a ball back into play as soon as the players have made their attempt on goal.

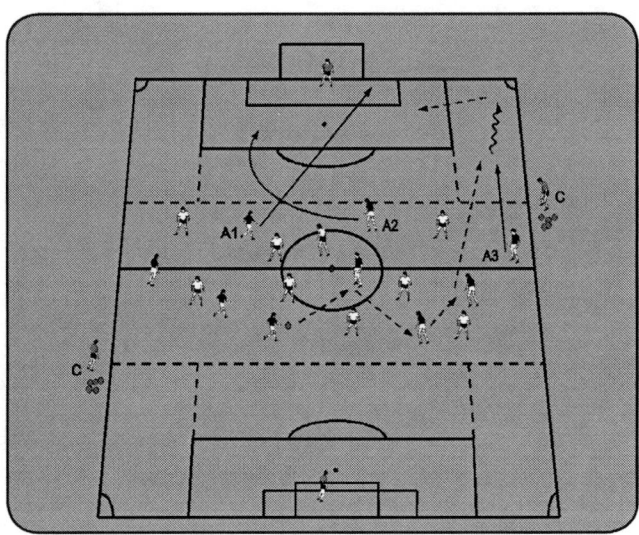

Chapter Five

Defending

This session was conducted by University of Nebraska Women's Head Coach, John Walker at the February 2005, WORLD CLASS COACHING International Coaching Seminar in Kansas City. The session focuses on Team Defending.

Ball Winning 7 v 7

In a 60 x 60-yard grid with goals at each end, teams line up 7 v 7 + 1. The game starts with the goalkeeper each time. The goalkeeper must throw or kick the ball in the air each time to create a 50/50 ball winning situation. Each team tries to score past opposition but points are also awarded for winning back the ball.

Coaching Points

- Defend high up the field
- Press the ball carrier
- Ball winning - interceptions, aerial, knockdowns and tackles
- 1 point for ball won, 3 points for actual goal
- Individual defending
- Communication
- Team organization

Progression(s)

- Play offside or not offside
- Play for 6 minutes or first team to 15 points

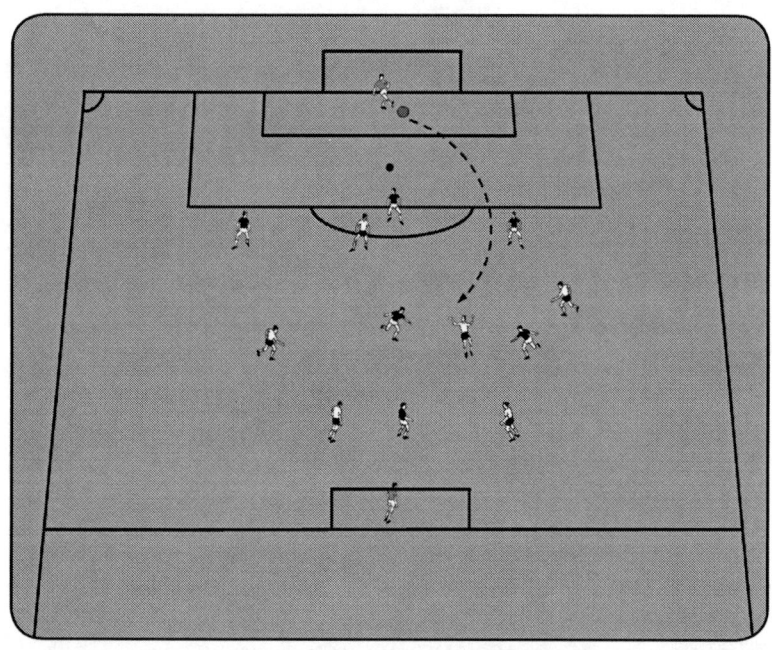

Team Ball Winning Competition

Two separate 50 x 50-yard grids side by side, with both areas having one goal, with two teams split (half of each team in each area). Half of team A defends in one area against team B. Half of team B defends in one area against team A. Two "passer's pass the ball into the attacking teams who are simply trying to connect passes. Defending teams must try and win the ball as quickly as possible and complete a pass. Teams compete against each other on each side to win the ball first.

Coaching Points
- Ball winning mentality
- Individual defending
- Immediate pressure on the ball
- 1 point for ball won, 3 points for actual goal
- Man-to-man or zonal defending
- Prevent forward from turning

Progression(s)
- Win a ball and complete two passes
- Win a ball and get a shot on goal or score a goal
- Double team only

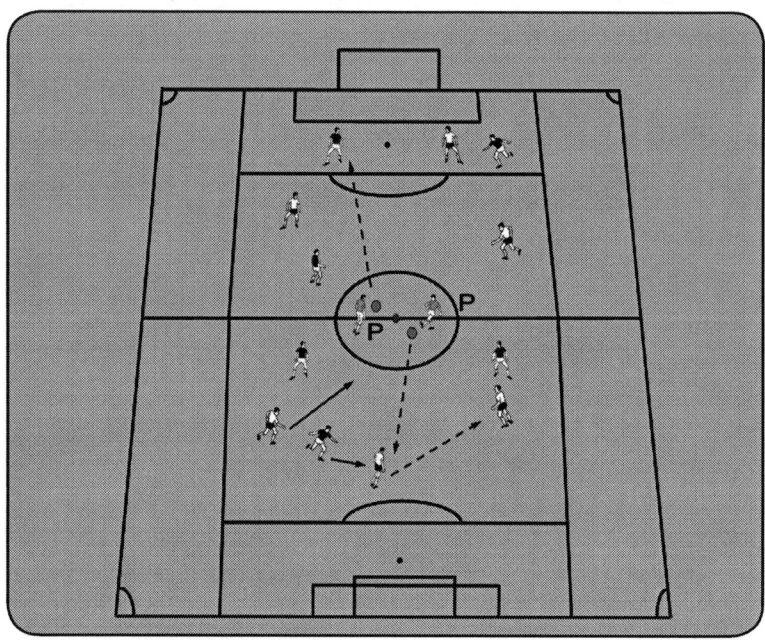

Front Half Defending And Transition

Using the front half of the field to one goal. Defending team lines up with two forwards, three midfielders, one stopper and two outside defenders. The attacking team lines up with four defenders, three midfielders and one forward. The defending team wins the ball and attacks the goal. The attacking team tries to hit targets and or dribble across half way line. The ball can start with either team to vary starting positions.

Coaching Points

- Starting positions - be compact
- Can you intercept?
- Preventing good open forward pass
- Can you prevent turn?
- Working backwards
- Defending against third man runs
- Individual defending at point of confrontation
- Double team opportunities
- Transition - Immediate pressure on the ball
- Wingback aggressiveness

Progression(s)

- Play two touch
- Rotate players positions and responsibilities

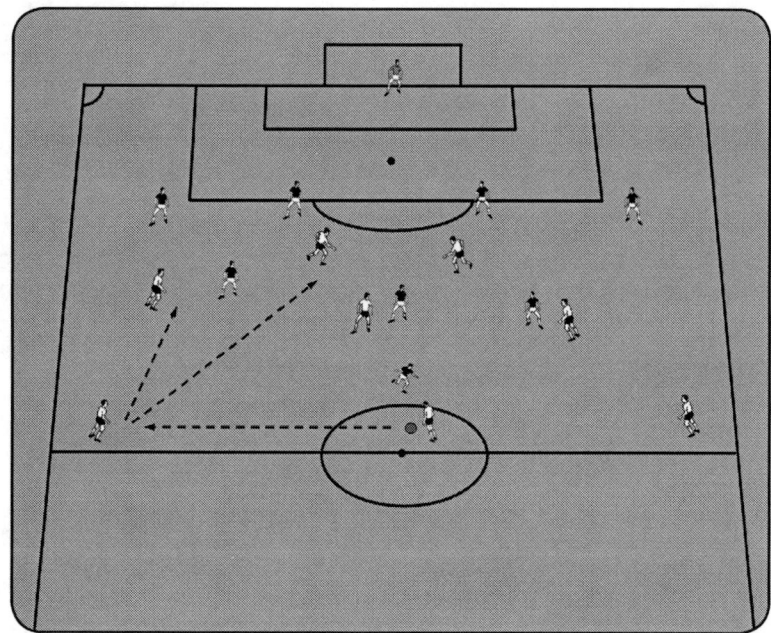

Back Half Defending And Transition

Use half a field with goals at each end. Both teams line up with two forwards, three midfielders and three defenders. The defending team defends the goal and wins ball and attacks goal on halfway line The attacking team tries to score in regular goal. Scoring is one point for a shot and three for a goal for the attacking team, three points for a goal for the defending team. The attacking team starts without outside fullback support. The defending team starts without striker being active defensively.

Coaching Points

- Starting positions - be compact - immediate
- Denying penetrative passes, shots, crosses etc
- Travel together - compact - position to intercept
- Reading when to drop and when to stay high
- Zonal sliding
- Defending against third man runs
- Individual defending at point of confrontation
- Team communication
- Transition/balance when ball is lost
- Mentality to deny dangerous passes, shots and crosses
- Box defending quality (marking, clearances, toughness)

Progression(s)

- Add fullbacks coming forward and striker being active defensively

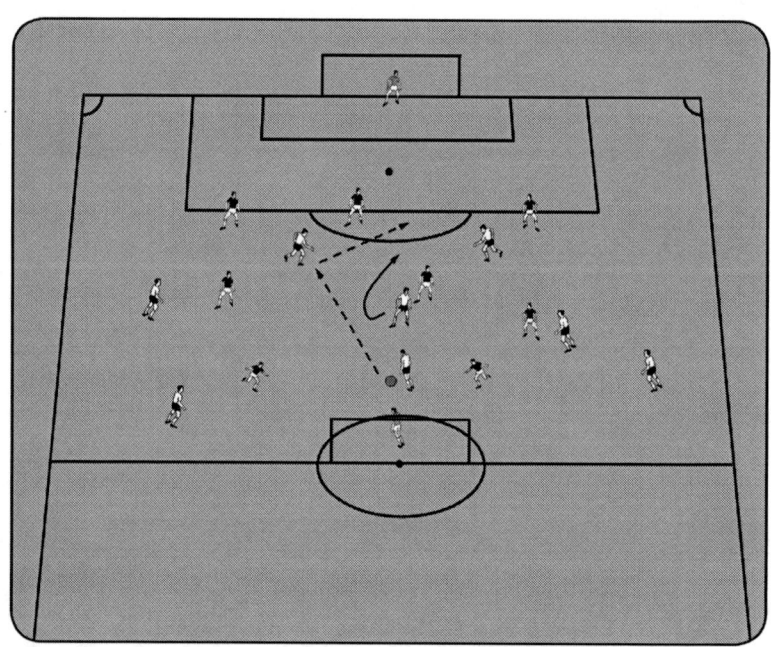

These games are a part of a defending session by then Sheffield United U15 coach, Sam Saif. Saif holds a EUFA "A" License and has over 15 years experience coaching at youth academies for professional clubs in England.

Pressing

Two teams play 6 v 6 for 45 seconds using approximately one quarter of a regular field. One player rests and counts the interceptions and losses of possession as a result of the "pressing tactic". X's (the majority) play possession football. O's (the minority) press to destroy possession. Change teams and roles at the end of 45 seconds.

Coach starts each game by passing to team in majority. O's press as a team to destroy possession by forcing the ball out of playing area. Coach immediately releases another ball to the majority. At the end of 45 seconds, count the losses of possession.

Coaching Points

- Who? presses the ball
- How? with what intention
- When? does the press begin
- Reaction/responsibilities of others
- Prevent the change of play

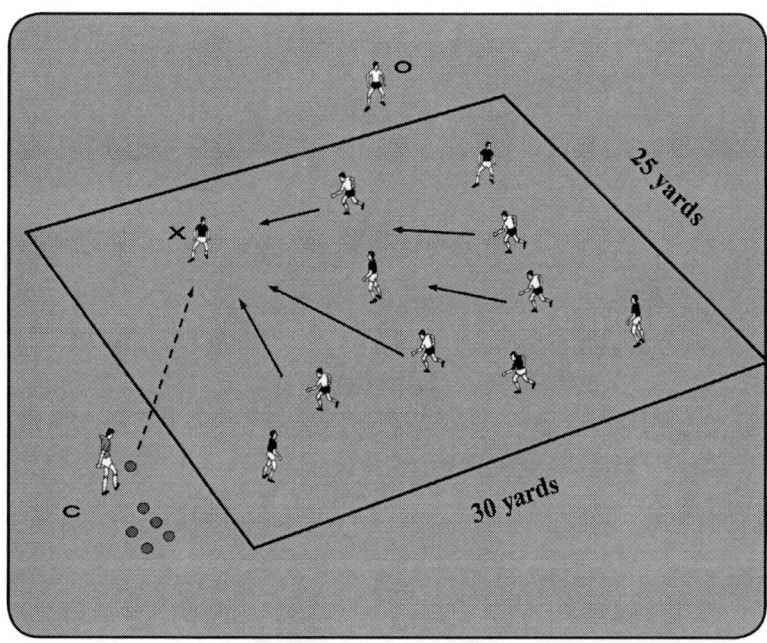

Pressing

Two teams play 6 v 6 , 7 v 7, 8 v 8, etc. Have a supply of balls behind each goal. Coach calls a color, and the GK can distribute to any of those players.

Coaching Points

- Team "out" of possession works on pressing
- Who? presses the ball
- How? with what intention
- When? does the press begin
- Reaction/responsibilities of others
     - Mark
     - Track
     - Cover
     - Recover

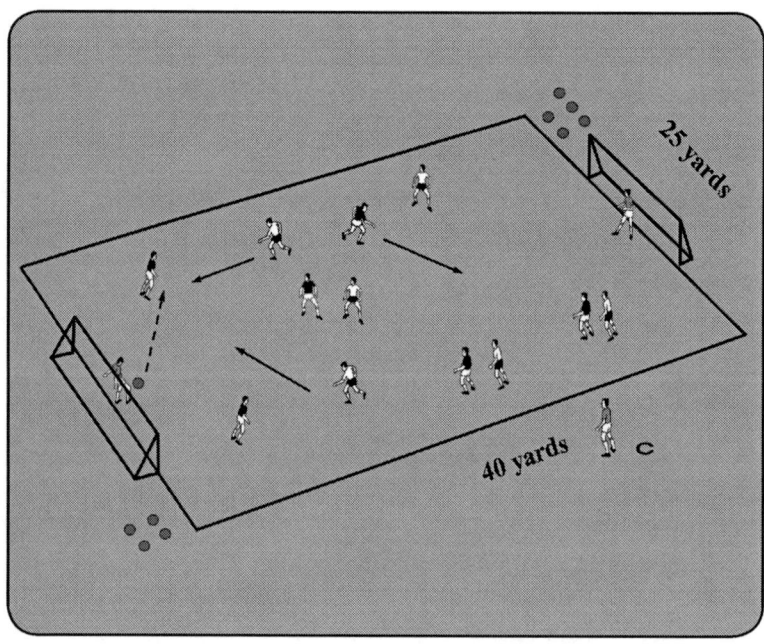

Man Marking

Two teams play 7 v 7 on a 40 x 70-yard field. Five pairs of players who mark on man-for-man basis. One sweeper on each team with three-touch limit and can play in own half only.

Coaching Points

- Who to mark?
- How to mark?
- Tight and loose marking
- Defending in 1 v 1 situations
- Responsibilities "off the ball"
- Defending against "combination play"
- Defending when the ball is played beyond you, towards your goal
- Defending for beaten in 1 v 1

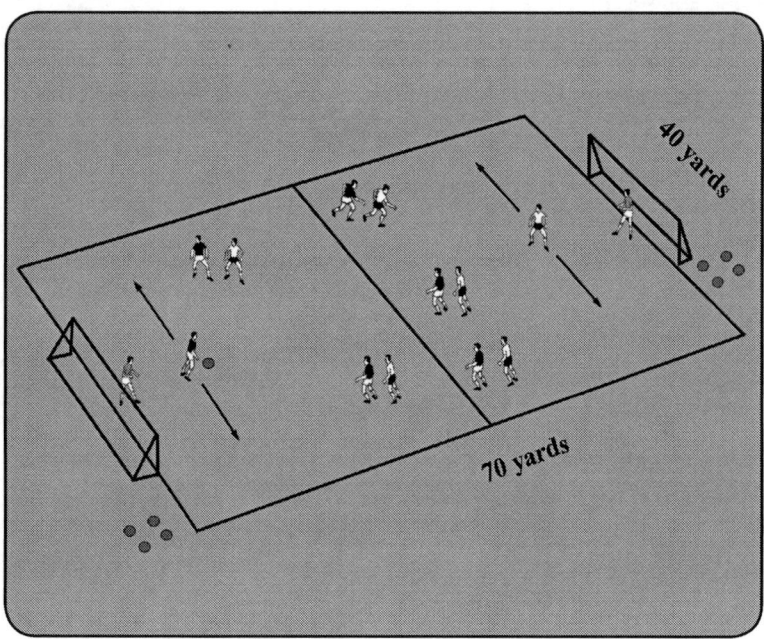

During my visit to England for the FACA Coaches Conference, I had the opportunity to visit the Crystal Palace Youth Academy. There I observed the training sessions of the U11, U15 and U16 teams. This game was part of a training session that was done in the evening, outdoors, on an artificial surface. The weather was windy with the temperature close to freezing.

Hand Ball Game

The coach used this game to get across defensive coaching points. The game was played in 20 x 20-yard area with two teams of four playing keep-away plus one neutral player. The ball was carried in the player's hands and they were allowed to run with the ball or pass it to teammates to avoid getting stripped of the ball. It was similar to basketball except the players didn't have to dribble the ball when they moved. The team not in possession tried to steal the ball or intercept a pass but were not allowed any real physical contact. To receive a pass from a teammate, players had to work hard to get open and find space. If the ball hit the ground, possession went to the other team.

Coaching Point

The coach stressed many individual defensive points.

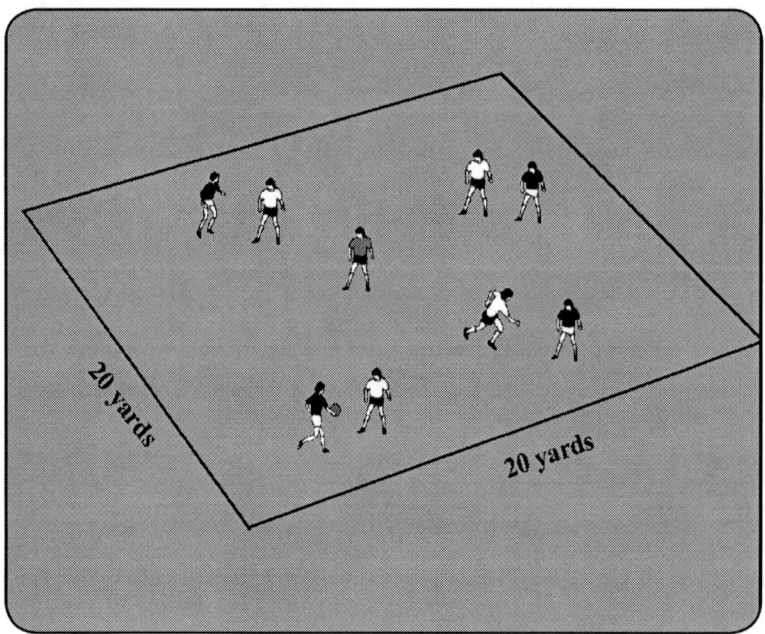

Progression #1

The game was progressed by adding cones to form two small goals as shown in diagram 21. To score a goal, players had to throw the ball in the air for themselves to head through the cones. Players could block the goal by swatting the ball away from the player as he is heading toward goal.

Progression #2

Each player pairs off with someone on the other team. Players can only steal the ball from their partner.

Progression #3

Now play with feet - be patient, players will make mistakes when playing at speed.

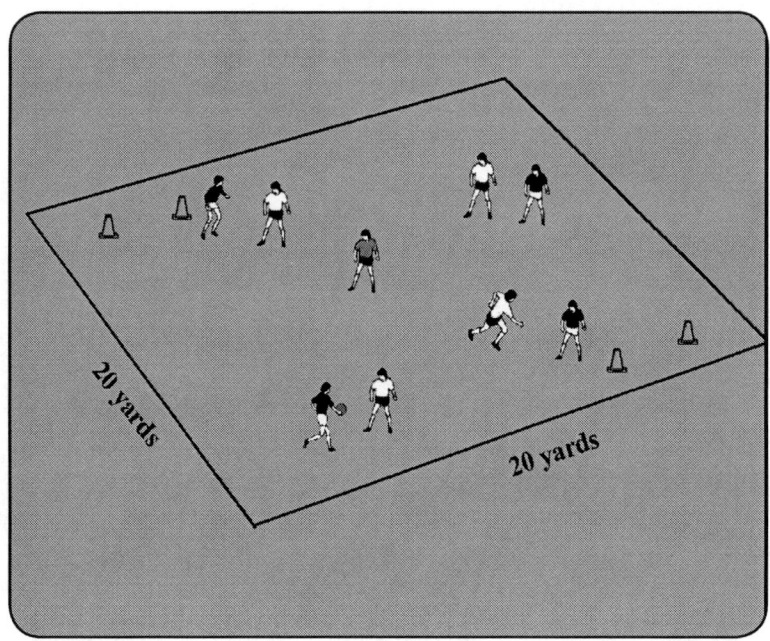

These games are part of a session contributed by Jeff Pill, then U.S. Women's National Staff Coach and U.S. Women's U18 National Team Assistant Coach. You can find more of Jeff's training sessions at www. eteamz.com/soccer/pills/jpill.htm

We needed to improve the team's ability to coordinate the defense of the back four and midfield four. Too many gaps were present, and, they had difficulty reading how, when, and where to put pressure on the ball. This activity addressed that concern well. It also gave the team confidence in the defending 'system' as this game showed them that they could play numbers down and still have success with their defending.

Activity One
The 'white team' attacks with all 11 players.
The 'dark team' can only defend with eight field players and a keeper.
If the 'dark team' wins the ball, the two strikers, who are waiting outside the marked line, can come back in to their own half and assist the team in getting the ball over the marked line.

Once this is done, the game is now reversed, with the 'darks' attacking against the 'lights' nine players (the two light strikers go and wait in their attacking half beyond their marked line).

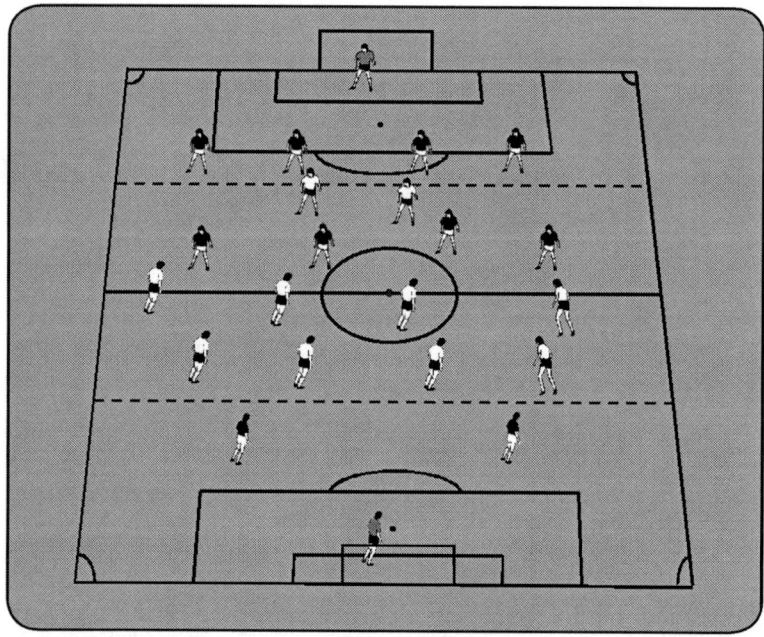

Activity Two

To help improve the coordinated defensive action of our front players with our midfielders, we played this activity.

Early on, our strikers had the tendency to charge after the ball, opening up a big gap between them and the midfielders.

As a result, their backs played the ball easily around us and were able to penetrate into our half.

The Game

6 v 7 plus a keeper.

The seven 'dark' players score a goal by dribbling over the half line.

The six 'light' players score by shooting in to the big goal.

This game was part of a sessions observed at the Sheffield United Academy by Ozzie White during a trip to the UK. Sam Saif conducted the session with the U15's.

Half Field Practice 5 v 5

Using one half a regular sized field, one large goal is placed at one end with five mini goals placed on the half way line. Five players attack the mini goals and must dribble the ball through to score a goal. Five players defend the mini goals and must attack the normal goal.

Coaching Points

- Defenders defending the mini goals must defend as a unit
- Apply pressure
- Make play predictable
- Provide pressure, cover, balance
- Move together when ball moves

Progression

- Rotate so both teams attack mini goals

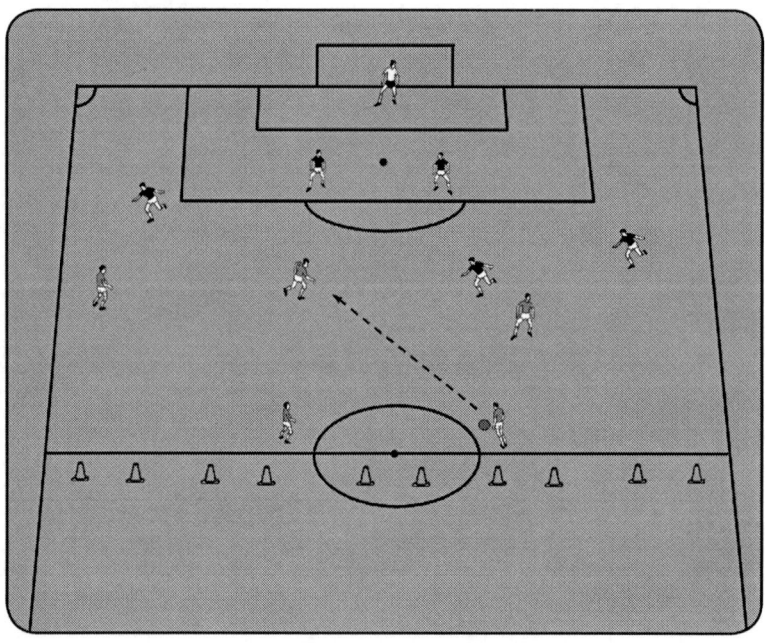

Contributed by Tony Carr, Youth Academy Director at West Ham United Football Club. Tony is considered a leading authority on coaching youth players game. Tony is also well known as the author of the book "Coaching Youth Soccer" which can be found on the West Ham United official web site - www.westhamunited.co.uk.

The following training session, *"Breaking Out Of Defense With The Ball"* is a practice I use quite often and was devised when our England international defender, Rio Ferdinand, was a youth team player and I wanted to encourage him to break out of defense with the ball. At this time we were playing with a five man defense. The session would begin with a general warm-up of jogging and stretching lasting about 20 minutes. This would be followed by a technique session of passing and moving in threes, progressing from short to longer passes.

The main session would last for one hour with short breaks for coaching points and drinks to re-hydrate the players. The session progresses from 3 v 2 in each half to adding midfielders and splitting the field into thirds. The final session becomes a more game-like situation with 3 v 2 in each end third and 2 v 2 in the midfield area.

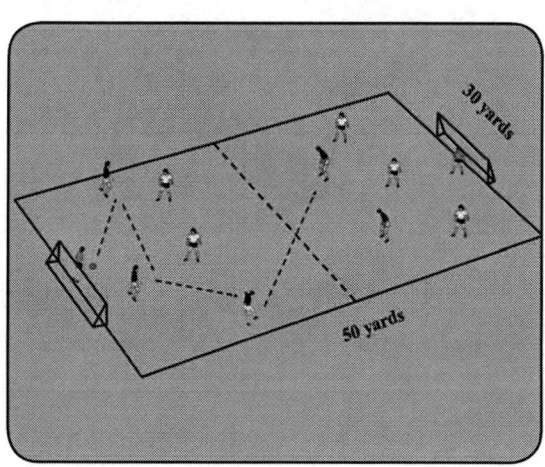

Session One
Organize the players in a 50 x 30-yard area with a half-line marked as shown in diagram 1. Play 3 v 2 in each half. The goalkeeper begins by throwing the ball to a defender. All three defenders must touch the ball before they can pass it into the other half to one of their forwards.

Coaching Point
Having the goalkeeper distribute the ball to the defenders makes the defenders comfortable in receiving the ball and gives them practice in playing the ball out of defense.

Progression

Allow one defender to dribble the ball to the attacking half creating a 3 v 3 situation. If the defending team wins the ball, the other team must recover into their starting defensive positions.

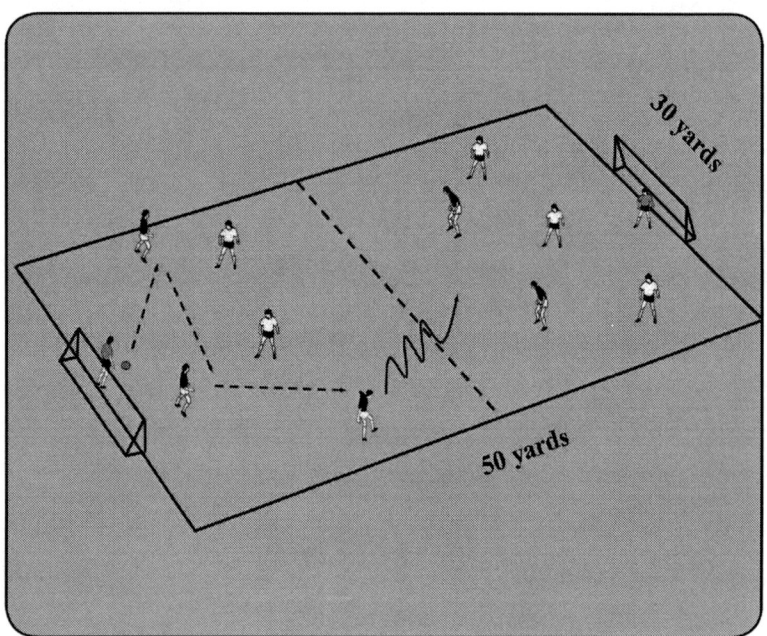

Session Two

Progress to a 60 x 40-yard area. Play 3 v 2 in each end third and 2 v 2 in the middle third.

As in session one, a defender can break into the central area. He then has two choices:

A. If he is not challenged by a midfielder from the defending team he can take the ball himself into the attacking third creating a 3 v 3.

B. If a midfielder from the defending team challenges him, as D1 does in diagram 3, he can play the ball to the 'free' midfielder who runs into the attacking third and creates a 3 v 3.

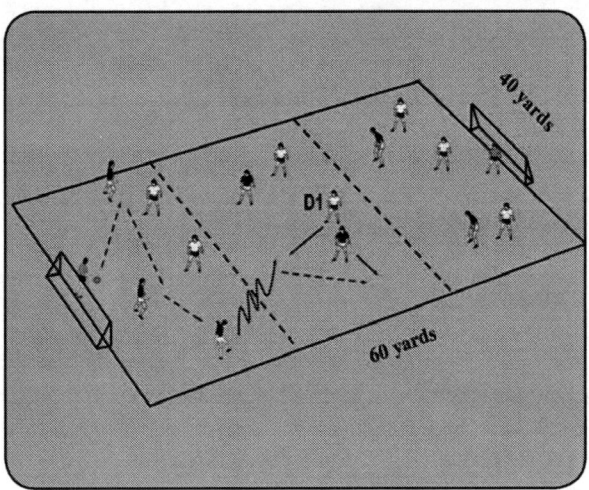

Progression

When moving into the attacking third from the midfield third, the player in possession has the option of passing to one of the two forwards or attacking the goal himself.

Only one player from each 'area' can break forward at any one time without being tracked by opposition.

Following the practice stages, we take away the restrictions of areas and play 'free' soccer but emphasize the disciplines of good defending and attacking principles.

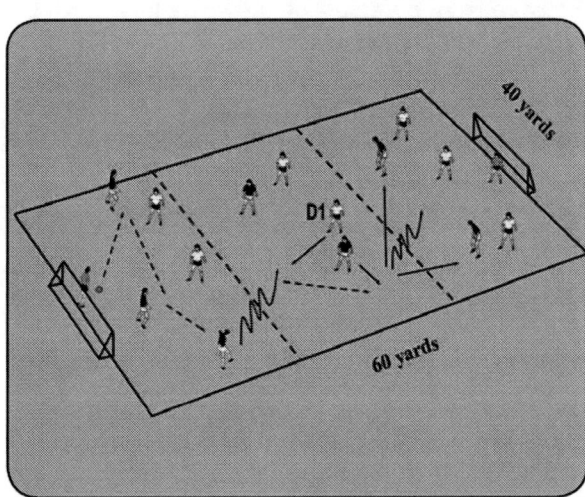

These games were contributed by Lars Svensson, then head coach of Lira Lulea BK. Svensson played soccer for over 17 years in his native country, Sweden, where he went on to coach the First Division club, Lira Lulea BK.

I prefer to play a 4-3-3 system with my teams. This transitions to a 4-5-1 formation when we are defending. The following are generic coaching points I use with all my defending training sessions.

Defensive Clearances
- When to play controlled possession or clear the ball out big and long is determined by the pressure on the player in possession.
- Push up as a team when clearing the ball or when the opposition is playing backwards.
- Put maximum height and distance on the clearances.
- If the opposition wins the ball back, stop pushing up and maintain a safe distance.
- Defend in two lines - defenders and midfielders. Two forwards should drop into midfield to make a 4-5-1 formation.
- Maintain a distance of approximately 12-15 yards between the defending line and the midfield line.
- Maintain aggressive pressure on the ball and keep your feet moving so that you are able to give support and cover.
- Switch from zone defense to man-for-man marking when the ball enters the penalty area.

Opponents In Uncontrolled Possession
- Strive to win the ball immediately.
- Tight aggressive, effective pressure on the player in possession.
- Cut off the passing lanes to nearby players.

Opponents In Controlled Possession
- Organize the defending and midfield lines immediately.
- Quick pressure on the player in possession.
- High pressure on players in the attacking half and low pressure on players in the defending half.
- The defensive line should be no deeper than the penalty area and no further forward than the half-line.
- Communication in order to organize.
- Stay tight and compact as a team.

Opponents Attacking Through The Middle
- Move players into the central area.

- Wide players should move inside.
- Make the team compact.

Opponents Attacking On The Wings
- The whole team 'slides' toward the wing.
- Establish tight pressure on that side of the field.
- Weak side players should drop back and into the middle.

Pressing/Defending
Organize a 40 x 30-yard field with cones marking out 10-yard wide goals on each end-line. Play 5 v 5 with the objective of trying to score by dribbling through the coned goal.

Coaching Points
- Communicate from behind
- Closest player to the ball should pressure
- Pressure quickly

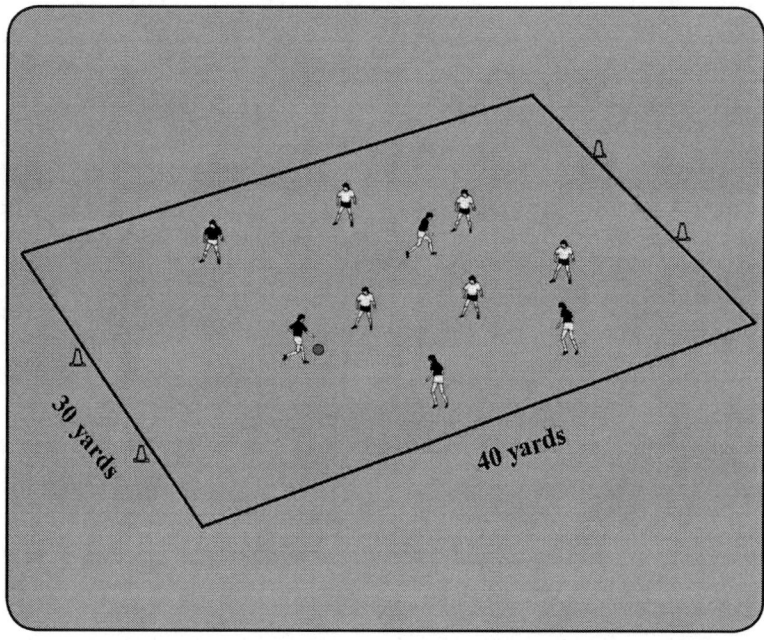

4 v 4 Defending

Play 4 v 4 on a 35 x 25-yard field. The team in possession has to drop two players to a deep position that can't attack and can only offer support. The other two players look to attack and score. The defending team must drop one player back as a goalkeeper. This means that there are always two attackers against three defenders. Change the players assignments often.

Coaching Points

- Cover the space behind each other
- Cover the line between the ball and your goal
- Communication

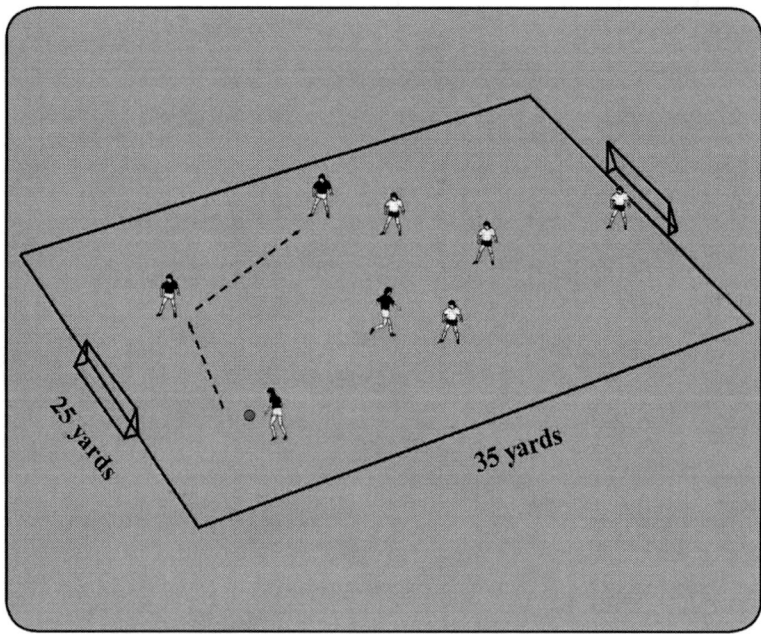

Defending With Midfielders
Play 6 v 6 on a 50 x 40-yard field with full size goals and goalkeepers. Organize each team to have three midfielders, two wingers and a center forward.

Coaching Points
- Force the player with the ball into your teammates
- Look for the next pass and react
- Communication

Progression
Increase the size of the field and number of players.

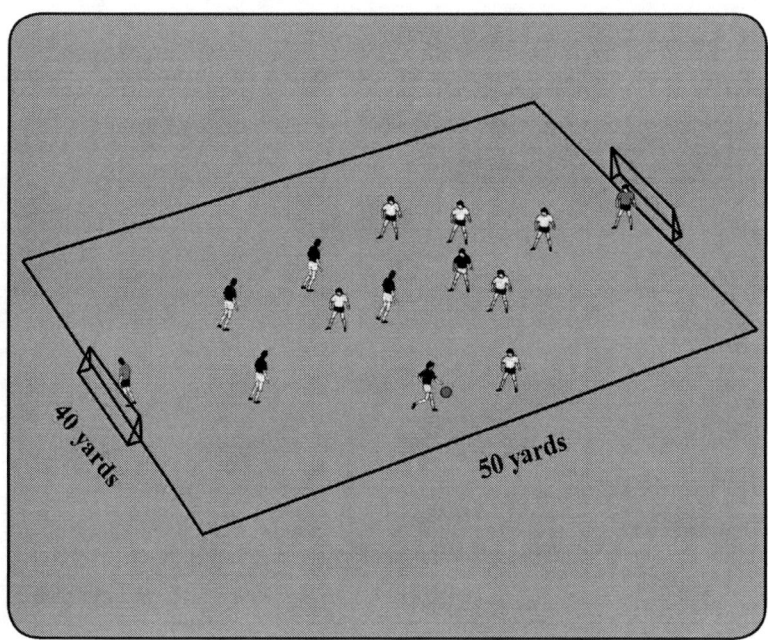

Tony DiCicco, coach of the U.S. Women's World Cup Winning Team of 1999, conducted two great sessions at the Coaches' Super Clinic conducted by Reedswain in New Jersey, February 3, 4 and 5, 2000. These games were done after individual defending practices that progressed to zonal defending with four players.

3 v 2 Small-Sided Game

This exercise progresses the session to defending in a small-sided game. The dark team attacks the two small goals on one end-line and the white team attacks the two small goals on the other end-line. Each team has two players in each half. There is also a neutral player in each half that plays for the team in possession making it 3 v 2 in each half. Progress this to using more players on a larger area.

Coaching Points

Use this small-sided game to develop the previous coaching points in a more game-realistic situation.

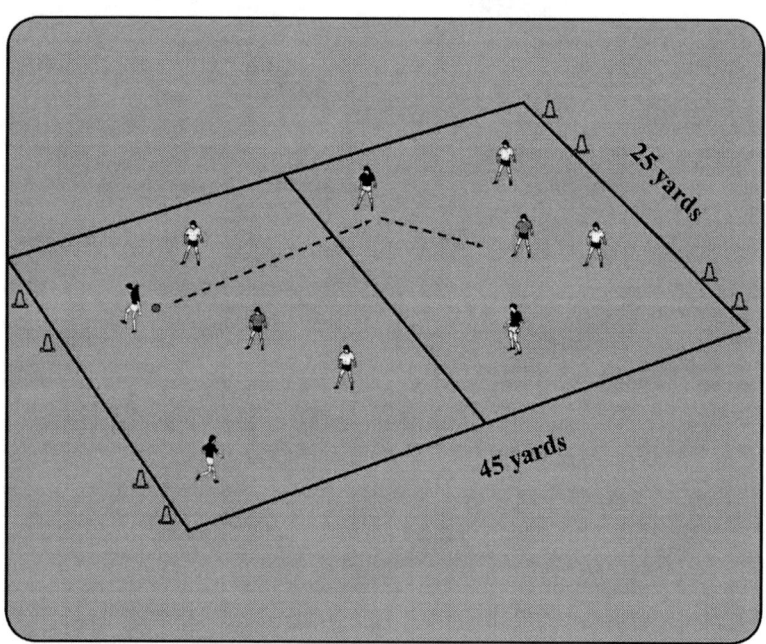

Midfield Zonal Defending

This exercise would normally be done on a 30 - 35-yard area across a full field. Play 4 v 4 plus a neutral player that plays for the team in possession.

Coaching Point

- Continue to develop all the previous coaching points
- Communication is vital to work as a unit
- Track the vertical runs of the attackers without the ball

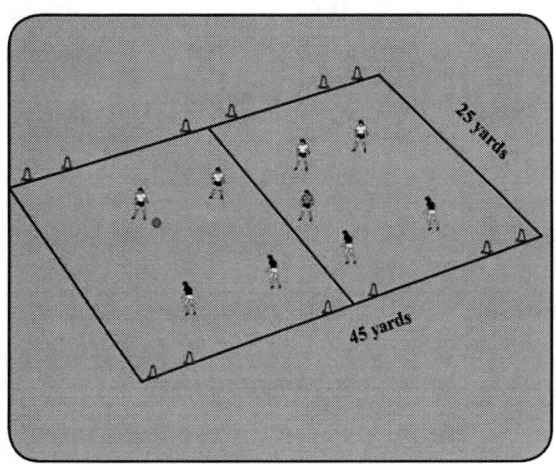

Progression

Two perimeter players for each team are added and are positioned on the attacking end-line. The perimeter players can be used by the attacking team and are limited to one touch. This forces the defending team to think about the spaces (gaps) between each player.

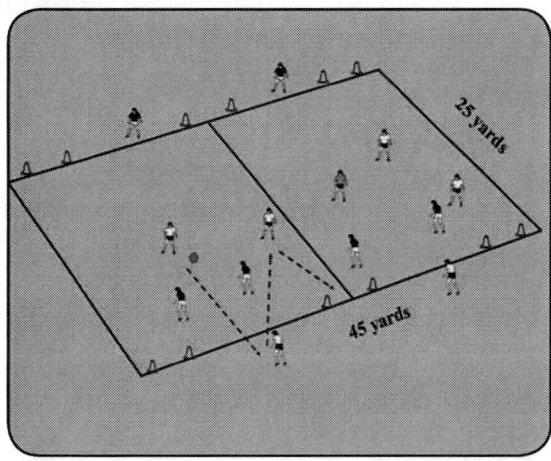

During my visit to England in October 2000, I was fortunate to spend a day at Liverpool F.C. with then Assistant Manager, Sammy Lee. This first team training session was done with team manager Gerard Houllier, and coaches Phil Thompson and Sammy Lee all involved. The objective of the training session was to work on closing down the opposition as quickly as possible. These games were played after a warm-up and some technical work.

Pressing The Opponent

Play 8 v 8 across the width of the field with the objective of playing the ball over the marked lines into the goalkeeper's hands without a bounce. The focus of the exercise is the closing down aspect of the game. Players are encouraged to quickly close down the ball and not be too concerned about the spaces or players behind them. If one team is successful in closing down, then the other team will be unable to get the ball to their goalkeeper.

Coaching Point

Communicate so that all players know who and when to close down.

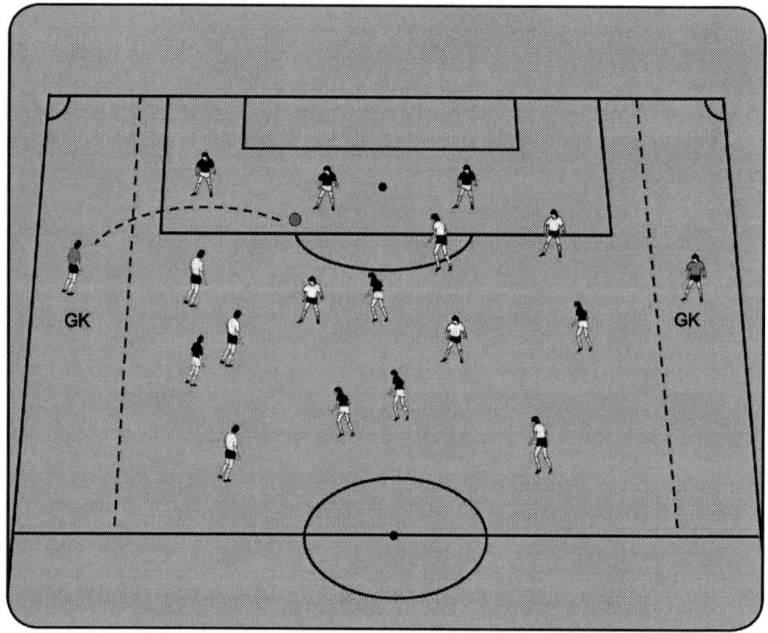

Progression

Using half a field, the objective again is to get the ball into the goalkeeper's hands, however this time from the defending half of the field. A team must complete five passes before being allowed to play a long ball into the goalkeeper.

Conditions

- Focus on individual defending techniques both from a forward and defender's point of view - body shape and position, forcing onto weaker foot, delay and slow down, etc.
- Off side is in effect
- Unlimited touches
- Two 8-minute halves

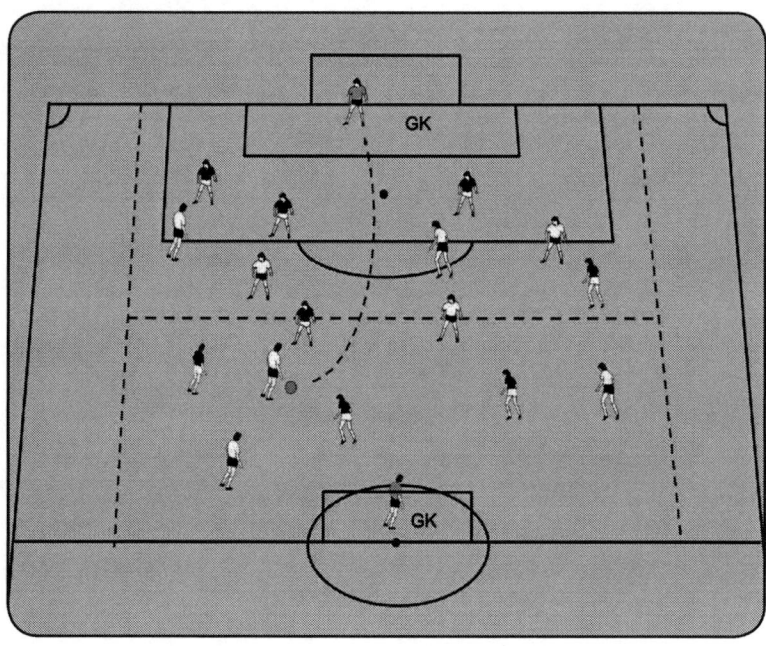

Chapter Six
Half Field Games

These games are part of a session submitted by Cristina Salamone, who played at Quinnipiac University. Cristina observed this A.C. Milan session in August 2004 when Milan were participating in the Champions Tour pre-season games. This training session was prior to Milan's game against Manchester United and included all the well-known players like Cafu, Crespo, Shevchenko, Seedorf, etc.

10 v 10 Keep-Away

A field is marked out by cones approximately 10 yards in from each touch line and three yards in from the halfway line and edge of penalty area. Two teams of 10 play keep-away with the objective of playing some short balls, then looking for long balls into the corners.

Example: Cafu playing at right back looks to hit the corners for Shevchenko and Crespo to run onto the ball.

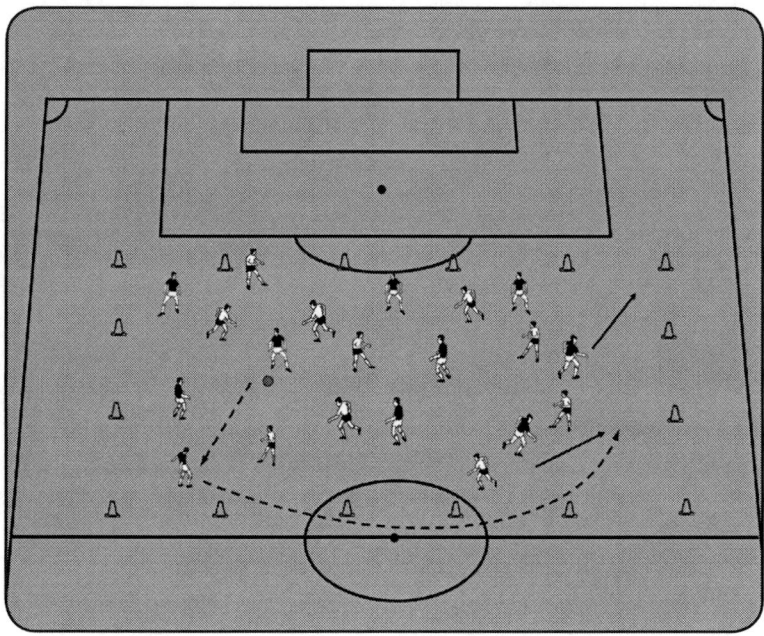

Progression - 11 v 11 Half Field With Keepers

Goals are now brought in and the game progresses to a half field 11 v 11 game with keepers in each goal. The focus is for the defenders to try and find Shevchenko and Crespo up top with long balls. When the balls are played long, fullbacks Cafu and Kaladze are encouraged to get forward in support or to make overlapping runs.

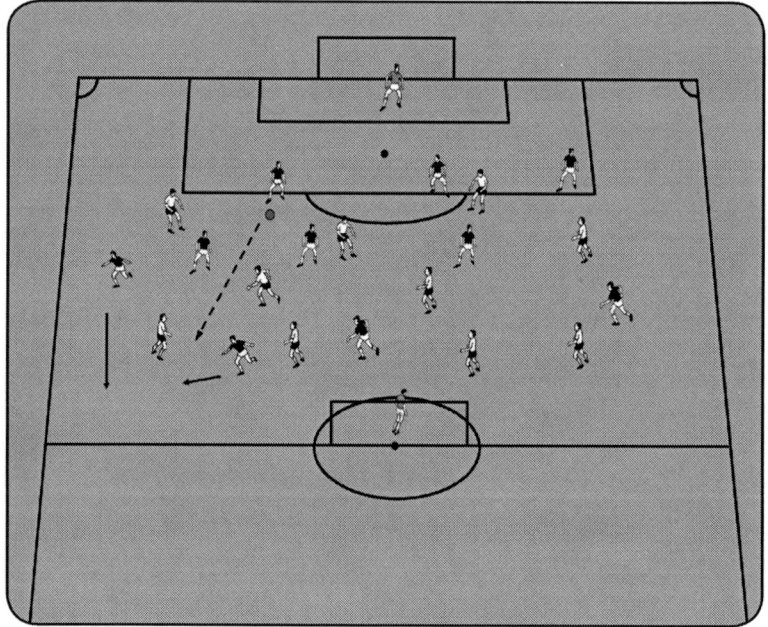

These games are submitted by Antonio Saviano. They are taken from the
U12 and U13 age group curriculum from the Perugia A.C. Academy in Italy.

Destroy The Castle
Using half a regular sized field and as wide as the 18-yard box, play 7 v 7. The
objective of the game is to knock down the cones positioned in front of each
goal. When the cone is knocked down it will be placed in front of the team's
own goal. The team that has more cones, or knocks all of the opponent's
cones down, wins.

Coaching Points
• Defensive and offensive collaboration
• Zone defense
• Precision play
• Precision shooting
• Body position

Progression(s)
Once the cones are all knocked down, teams can keep playing and the
last player on the team that does not have the cones anymore can be a
goalkeeper. If the team scores it will place back two cones in their goal.

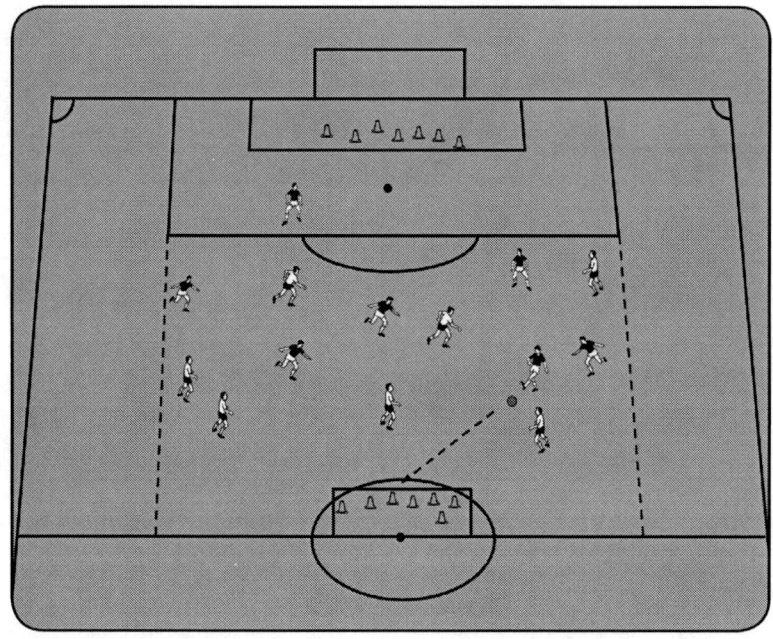

Choose The Goal

Using half a field with a grid 35 x 25-yard within. Two teams composed of five players each with the purpose to score in small goals of three yards wide. At the coaches signal, acoustic or visual, the objective changes and the team that has possession of the ball, based on the position on the field, will attack one of the regular size goals that are defended by a neutral goalkeeper. The other team will try to stop it.

Progression(s)

• Insert two more regular size goals behind the small goals

Coaching Points

• Quick conclusion in the goal
• Opening and marking
• Coordinative capacities
• Support
• Awareness

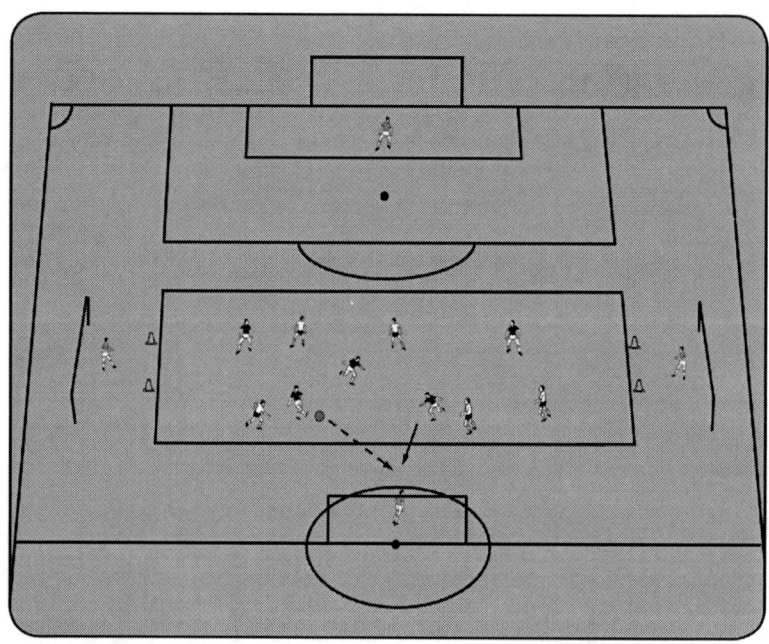

Game With Colors

Using half of a field, two teams composed of seven players each plus the goalkeeper compete. Each team is divided in two colors. If the goal is scored from a pass from a different color player on the same team, three points are awarded.

Progression(s)

The passes always have to come from a teammate by a different color. A team loses possession of the ball if passes with color sequence is not executed

Coaching Points

• Movement without the ball
• Defensive and offensive collaboration
• Conclusion in the goal
• Coordinative capacities
• Awareness

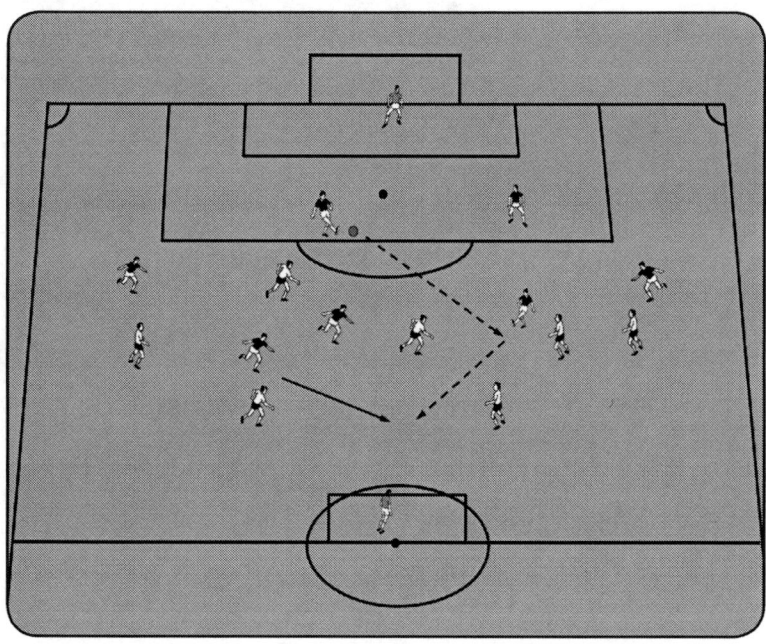

Everyone To The Goal

Using half of a field with goals placed at each end, play 7 v 7 plus
goalkeepers. The team that has the most number of players close to the goal
when a goal is scored gets the point.

Coaching Points
• Conclusion in the goal
• Opening
• Passing
• Coordinative capacities
• Offensive collaboration

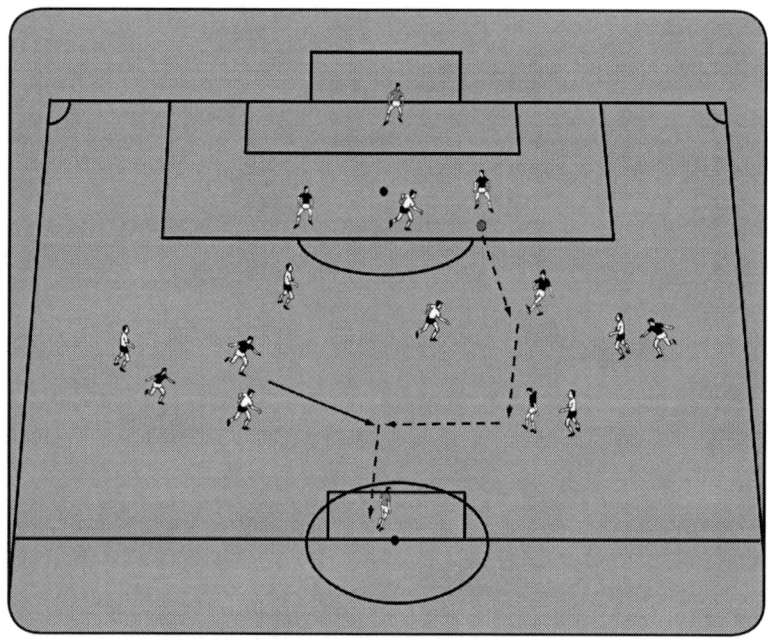

Cover Your Player

Using half of a field with goals placed at each end, play 7 v 7 plus goalkeepers. The objective is to score, but each component of the team must mark an opponent player.

Coaching Points
• Movement without the ball
• Marking
• Pressure
• Opening
• Passing
• Conclusion in the goal

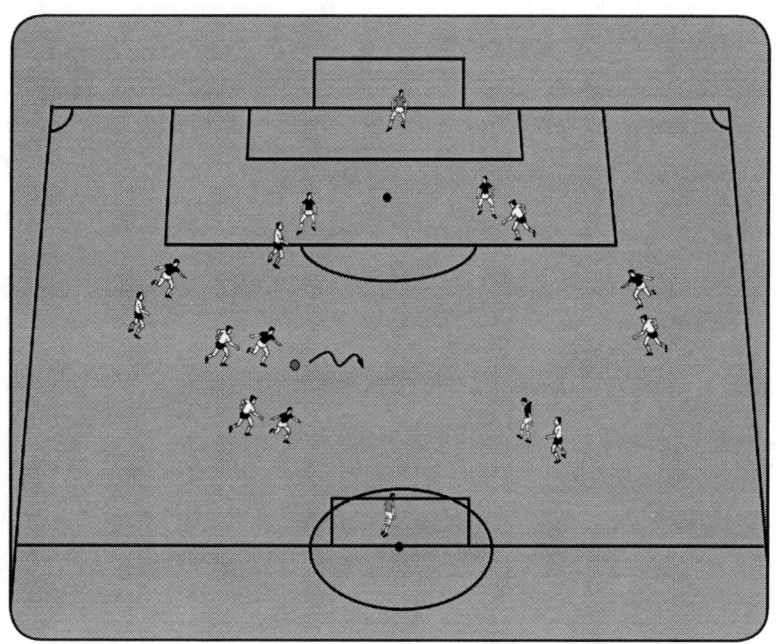

Everyone In The Half

Using half of a field with goals placed at each end, play 7 v 7 plus goalkeepers. The objective is to score, but the goal will be valid only if all the players of the attacking team are inside the attacking half.

Coaching Points

- Defensive and offensive collaboration
- Communication
- Conclusion in the goal
- Movement without the ball
- Awareness
- Offside

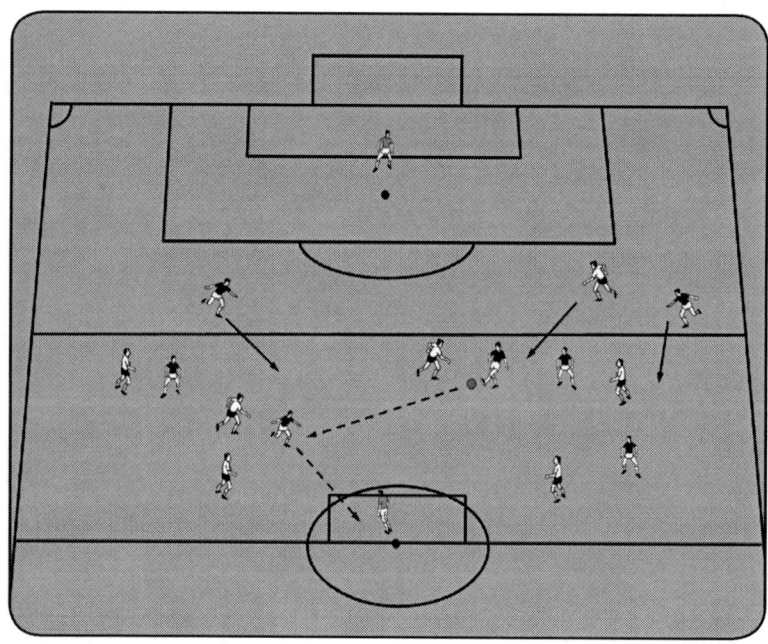

These games were part of sessions conducted by then Canadian Women's National Team Coach, Even Pellerud, at the WORLD CLASS COACHING International Coaching Seminar in Kansas City, February, 2005.

4 v 4 With Focus on Intensity
In a 40 x 30-yard field with goals at each end, two teams play 4 v 4 with a supporting target player by each goal post. A ball is played into the middle by a goalkeeper and the game begins.

Coaching Points
• Decision making - Needs to be quick
• High pressure
• Offensively - First pass forward, direct play
• Diamond shape
• Open up passing lane
• Diagonal runs

Progression(s)
• Two-touch only
• One-touch finishes
• Target players - One touch only

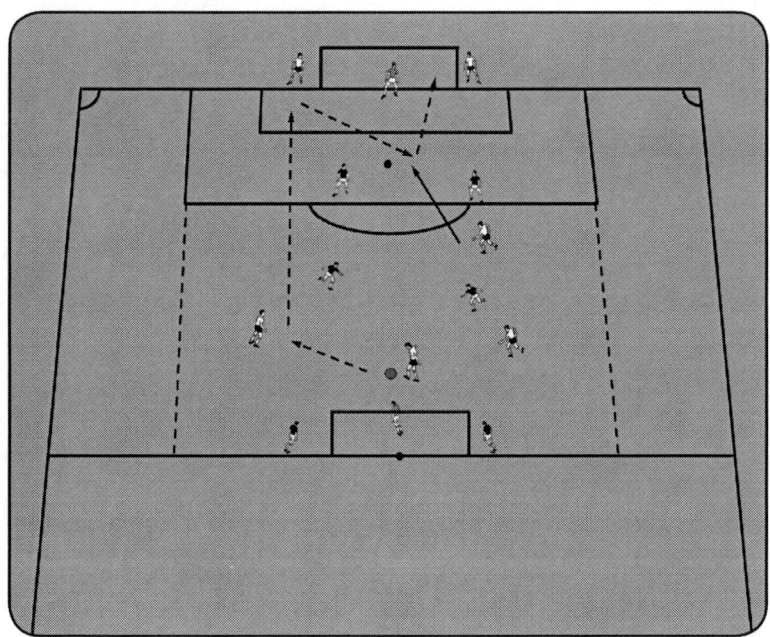

4 v 4 + 4 v 4

Using the same 40 x 30-yard field with goals at each end. Each team has four players on the inside and four supporting players on the outside.

Coaching Points
- Decision making
- Speed of play
- High pressure
- Diamond shape
- Open up passing lane
- Angles
- Diagonal runs

Progressions
- Two-touch only
- Target players - One touch only

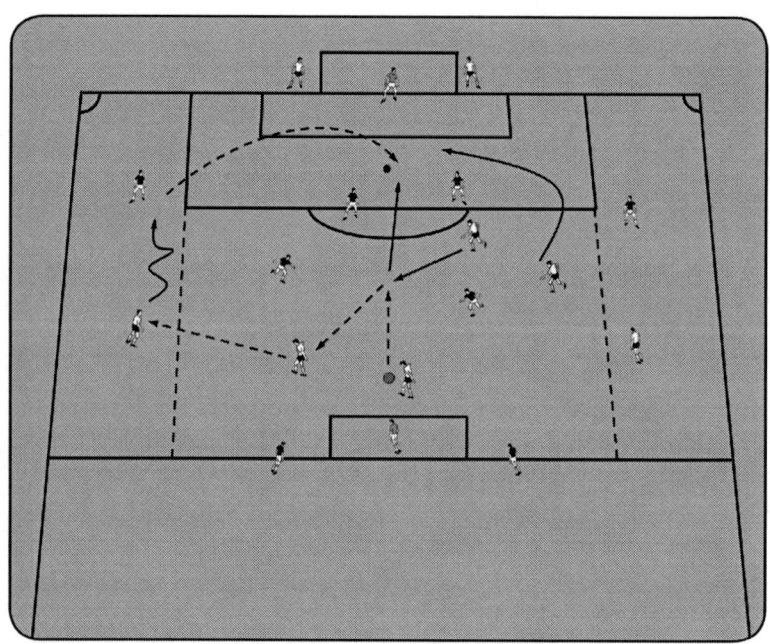

Crossing & Finishing - 5 v 5 + 2

Using a 60 x 40-yard field area, two full-sized goals are placed at each end. Two teams of five compete with two neutral players, one on each sideline. A ball is played in by a goalkeeper and the game begins. Goals can only be scored from a cross by neutral player.

Coaching Points

- Unlimited touches
- Encourage wide play early
- Always be dynamic
- Wide players to cross early and often

Progressions

- Rotate positions
- Two touch only

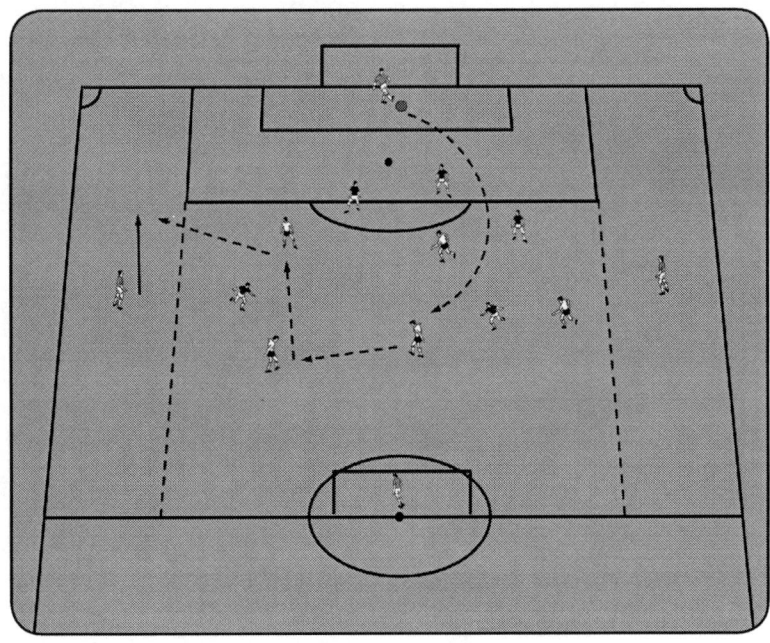

9 v 9 High Pressure Defense

On a small 40 x 40-yard field with goals at each end, two teams of nine players compete. A ball is played in by a goalkeeper and each team must defend high up the field to win back possession. After a goal is scored, the game is restarted with the goalkeeper.

Coaching Points
- No offside
- High pressure - All players
- Create problems for defensive team

Progressions
- Allow offside
- Restrict touches

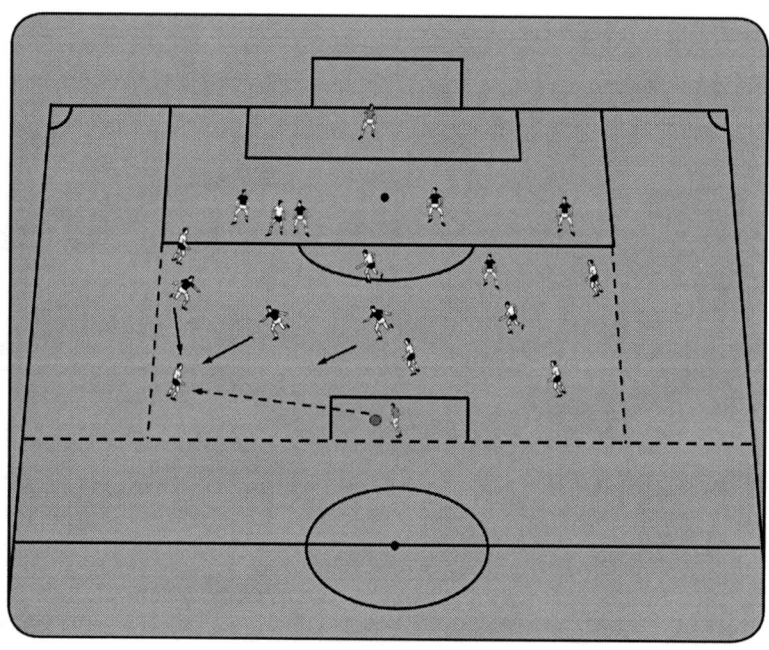

Mike Smith is one of the world's most experienced international coaches. To date he has coached teams in 212 international games. From 1974 to 1980 he was the manager of the Welsh National Team. From 1985 to 1988 he was manager of the Egypt National team where he won the African Nations Cup and the African Olympics. Mike went on to work with Wolverhampton Wanderers of the English First Division.

Half-Field Game

Coaches should develop all the previous situations in a variety of games. Playing 6 v 6 or 7 v 7 across half a field will produce many situations for the coach to observe and develop. Don't have offside in effect but protect the goalkeepers by insisting on one touch finishing only. The players are encouraged to run with the ball when they get the opportunity.

In the example in diagram 23, A1 passes to A2.
A2 has space so he runs with the ball at D2 and makes a decision to pass to A3, A4 or continue his dribble. In this example he passes to A3.
A3 has space, so he runs forward and is defended by D3.
Again, a decision has to be made. A3 can continue to dribble or pass wide to A4 or A5.
If A5 receives the ball, he can attack the goal and shoot.
If A4 receives the ball he can attack the end-line and deliver a low hard cross.

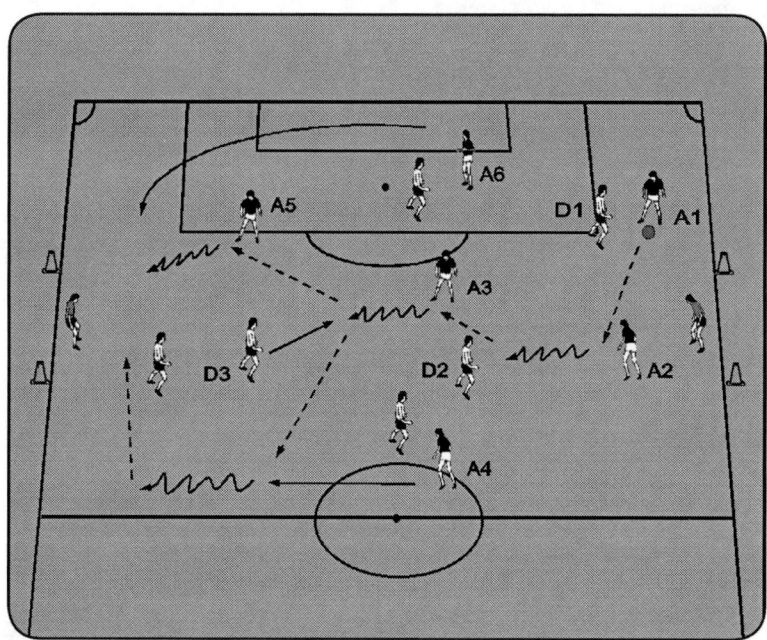

This game allows the players to examine their route to goal. However, if the A players lose possession, the B players must now attack by running the ball out of defense at opposing players. Then the question is, how do the A players respond? Do they run back? Where do they run to?

Coaching Point

The speed of movement of the counter-attack is critical in giving the attack by the B players superior numbers and exposing the A players.

Conclusion

- Many small-sided games are used to improve the technical qualities of the first touch, passing, support, movement, etc. But not many games are focused on running with the ball and attacking your opponents quickly.
- Most small-sided games are neat and tidy, mistakes are rare and usually involve play around the 'final pass'.
- Change the focus for the players so that not only do they have to win or intercept the ball, they then have to travel with it as fast as possible into the spaces that are available.
- Communication is vital because every player on each team must recognize their role at any moment of the game.
- I work with 15-16 year old players who really get up a 'head of steam' during these sessions.
- This session has all the decisions you will find in a game and they are recreated in a controlled way.

This game was part of a session contributed by Scott Placek, Director of Senior Programs, Longhorns Soccer Club, Austin, TX. This article is from a training session of the FK Teplice U18 team.

Field Training
Play 8 v 8 + GK on a half field. The dark team of eight attack the goal with the goalkeeper and the white team of eight attack a small three yard goal made of cones, which does not have a keeper. This was played for about 15 minutes and then was changed to 8 v 6 + GK.

Observations
The players were not given any touch restrictions, but played rather quickly. The players worked very quickly to free a teammate into space. Once free, the player quickly pushed the ball forward. The teams seemed to be looking for opportunities to score from either low driven balls which were played backwards or were sent in diagonally to players making hard diagonal runs toward the center of the goal. The players often demonstrated good use of one-touch passing in tight areas to unbalance the defense and free a teammate to play forward.

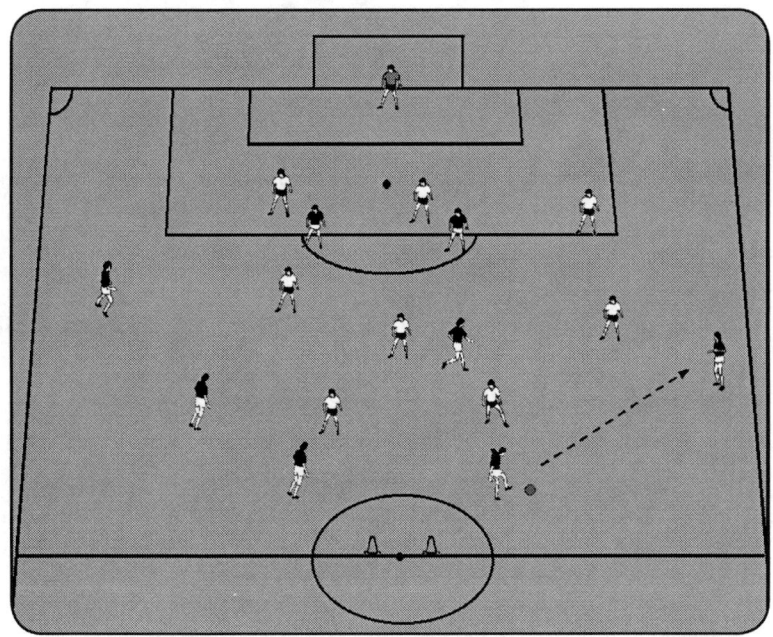

This game as a part of a practice conducted by Steve Heighway, the Director of the Liverpool Youth Academy and the U17 and U19 youth team coaches, Dave Shannon and Hugh McCauley. There were a total of 21 players from the two teams. This practice followed a long weekend break for the players with no games, so an element of conditioning was involved.

Half-Field Game
Play 11 v 11 across a half-field. The offside rule is in effect only over the lines that are marked 15 yards from goal. Play two 15-minute halves.

Observations
The game was played at a quick pace and was very competitive. The coaches stopped play only a few times and were very quick and firm with their coaching points.

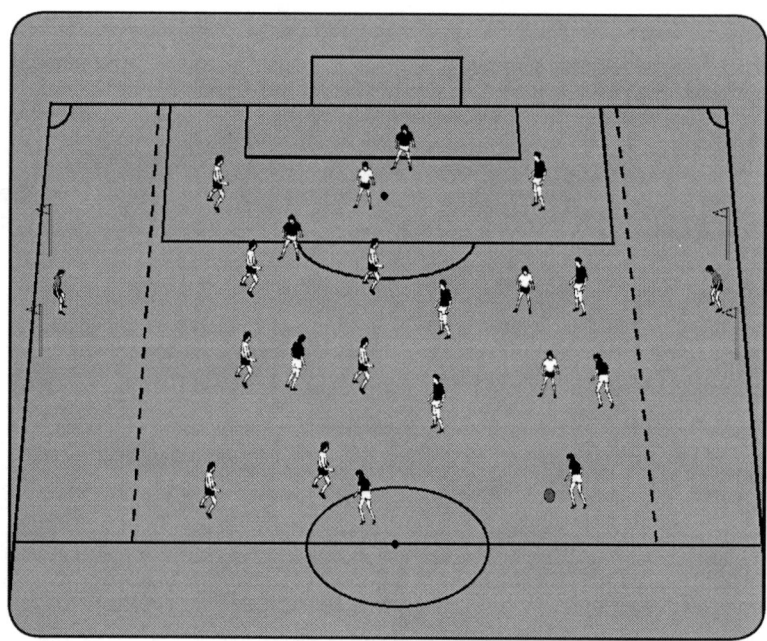

*These games are part of a pre-season training session with Bob Bradley
then head coach of the Chicago Fire. As observed at Orlando, Florida, 2001.*

Game One

The team is organized into a 9 v 9 situation (as shown in diagram 114) played
in the area between the 18-yard line and the half-line with either small goals
or cones. Balls are lined up on the sides of the field to keep the game flowing.

General Points

Players are limited to two-touch with a one-touch finish. Throw-ins are played
as normal and the coach keeps the score. Different conditions such as 10
passes equalled a goal, or a goal counts as double, or five goals wins the game
are introduced at various stages throughout the session.

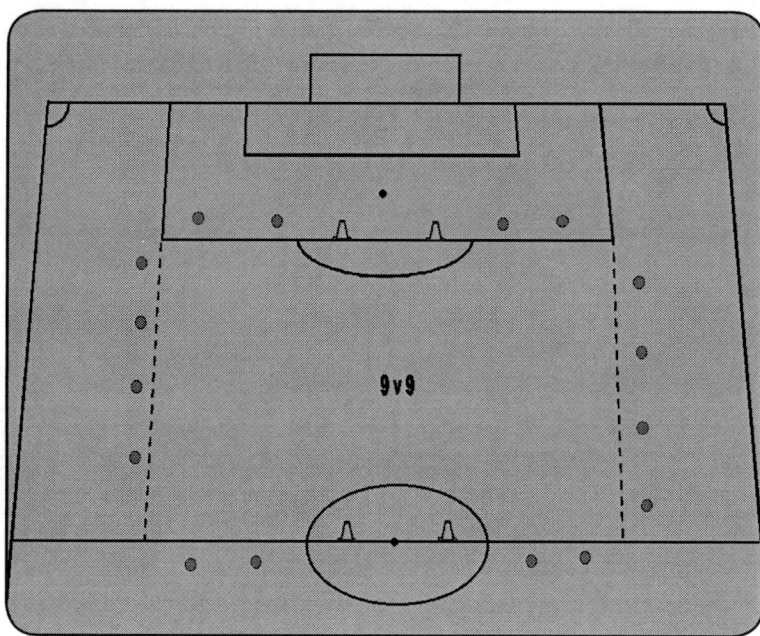

Progression

Now play is 8 v 8 in the same area with goalkeepers and full-size goals as shown in diagram 115. Unlimited touches are allowed, with normal throw-ins played. However, if one team wins three corners, they are given a penalty kick. No corners are taken and a goalkeeper starts with the ball.

Points

The coached stressed to the defenders to keep moving up and condense the play thus denying the opposition any space to play in.

The game lasted approximately 25 minutes and was followed by a warm-down jog and team stretch.

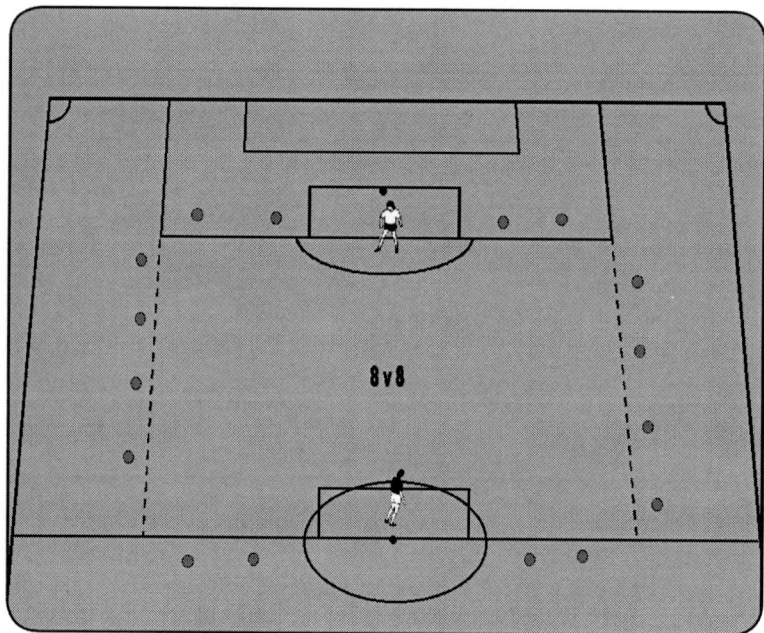

This game is part of a possession practice contributed by Ken Fogarty, former assistant coach, Kansas City Wizards.

Half-Field 9 v 9

Place nine sets of small goals using cones or flags on a half-field. Play 9 v 9. Goals can be scored three different ways.

- Ten consecutive passes
- A player dribbling through a goal
- A player passing through a goal to a teammate

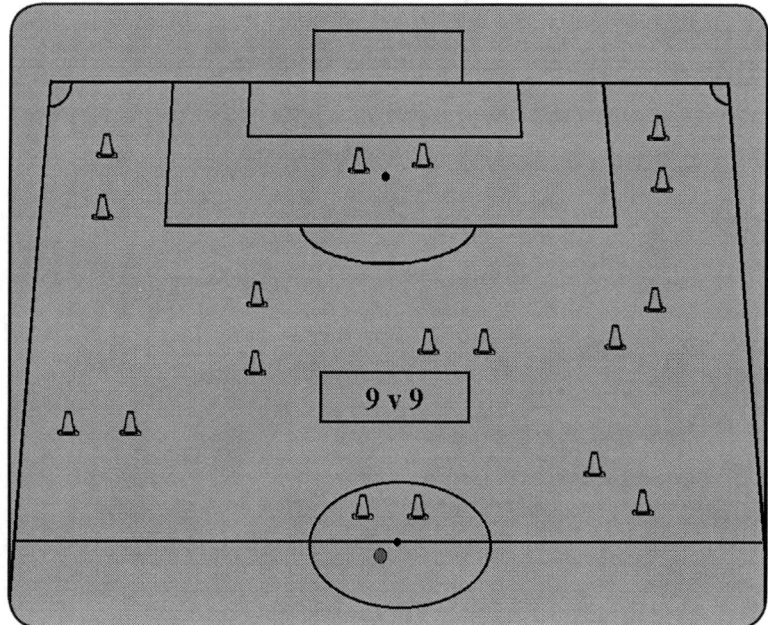

In February 1999, I was fortunate enough to spend a day with David Williams, who was the youth team coach at Manchester United at the time. As usual, it was a pleasure to observe Williams work with his players. On this day, the players trained in the morning and afternoon. The morning was a passing and possession session. This is the small-sided game at the end of the session.

Half-Field Game

Mark a field with lines extending from the edge of the penalty area to the half-line as shown in diagram 6. Use full size goals and goalkeepers. Play 5 v 5 + 1. A goal can only be scored with a one-touch shot. If the ball goes out-of-bounds, play is restarted with goal-kicks, throw-ins or corner-kicks. Start by playing three-touch. The coach was constantly asking his players to track the other teams' players when they made forward runs.

Progressions
- No restrictions - players are now encouraged to run with the ball if they have a chance. Still one-touch finish to score.
- Each team is shaped in a 2-2-1 formation. Maximum two touches. One touch is used if possible. If two touches are used, the second touch must be a forward touch.
- Add a player and play 6 v 6, no restrictions.

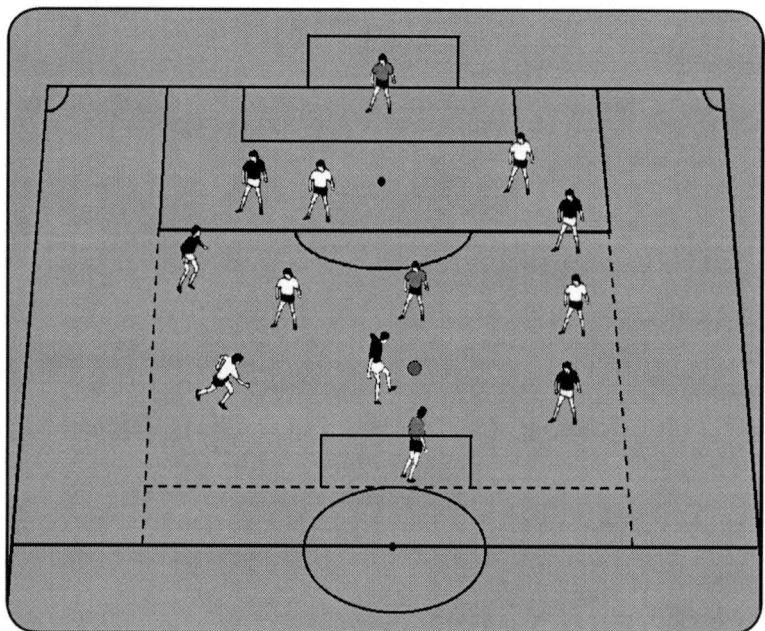

Chapter Seven

Full Field Games

This game is part of a session that focuses on finding and connecting with the target players through precise passing. The session was conducted by coaches Nicu Lazar and Alexander Szasz at F.C. Petrolul's U19 training camp in 2003.

Use a full field divided into three zones. The middle area is 20-yards wide and contains two target players who compete 1 v 1 for possession of the ball. The rest of the players are inter-passing in their zones (challenging each other heavily) trying to get the ball to their target player for which a point is awarded.

Variation
The players in the two zones are not allowed to tackle their opponents, only intercept.

Coaching Points
- Five to ten minutes of play, followed by some stretching
- Precise passes, putting spin on the ball
- Quick control and quick assessment of situations

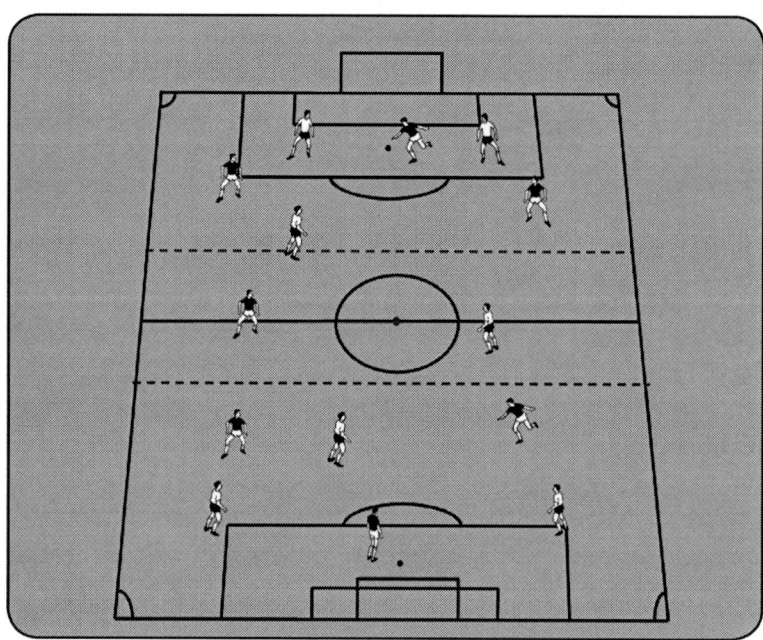

This game is part of a session contributed by Richard Hudson, who was the head coach of the New Zealand First Division team, AFC Manawatu. This article focuses on passing and possession.

Full-Field Game

Organize two teams of eight players (including goalkeepers) on a full-field. Mark the field with lines extending down the field from the sides of the penalty area as shown in diagram 67. This game can be used to get across all the coaching points from the previous drills in a more game-like situation. Special focus can be given to playing out from the defensive third, options and choices of midfielders and various attacking formations.

Coaching Points

- Positioning of defenders when goalkeeper has possession
- Clearance of space by pushing forward of midfielders when goalkeeper has possession
- Distribution of the goalkeeper
- Passing decisions from the defenders - do they pass short to a midfielder or long to a forward
- Midfielders must position themselves for a pass from the defenders or a lay-off from the forwards
- Midfielders decision to run with the ball to exploit space or pass
- Movement by the forwards to receive the ball from defenders or midfielders
- Decisions of the forwards to turn, dribble or pass to a supporting player

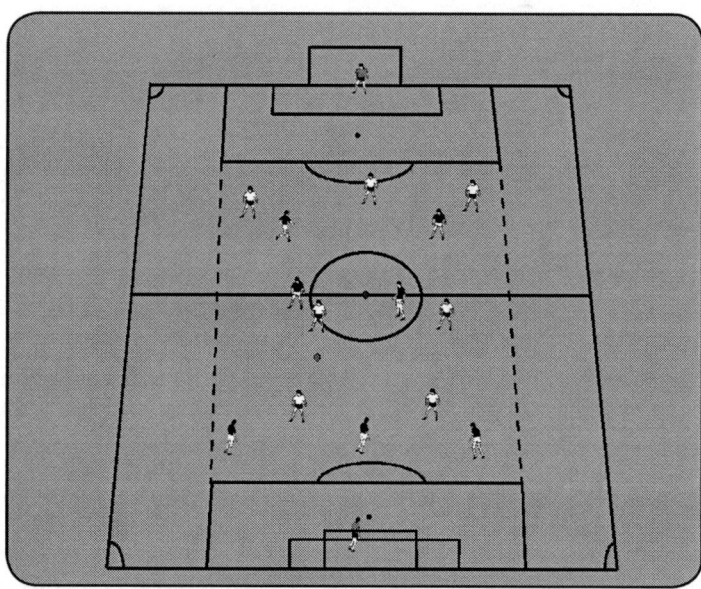

This game is part of a session submitted by Alexander Szasz, Director of Coaching for ESA of the USA. This session was conducted by Constantin Moldoveanu, Director of Youth Development at FC Petrolul Ploiesti of the Romanian First Division. The practice focuses on maintaining possession and applying quick pressure as a group in the defensive zone.

3/4 Field Game

Mark a 3/4 size field with lines extending from the penalty area and the goals on the 18-yard line as shown in diagram 73. Play 3 v 3 plus goalkeepers in each half. The players must stay in their own half. The goalkeeper starts the game by passing to one of his defenders. The objective for the defenders is to complete a pre-determined number of passes in their own half. The forwards attempt to win possession and mount a quick counter-attack on goal. If the defenders achieve the pre-determined number of passes, they get two points. The attackers get one point for an attempt on goal and two points if they score. The defending team can pass the ball to their teammates in the other half if they have no passing options in their own half. The defenders on one half are teamed with the attackers in the other half and combine points against the other team.

Coaching Points

• Forwards should defend as a team and not individuals
• If the forwards are unable to win possession, their next option is to force the defenders into passing to the opposite half before they reach their set number of passes

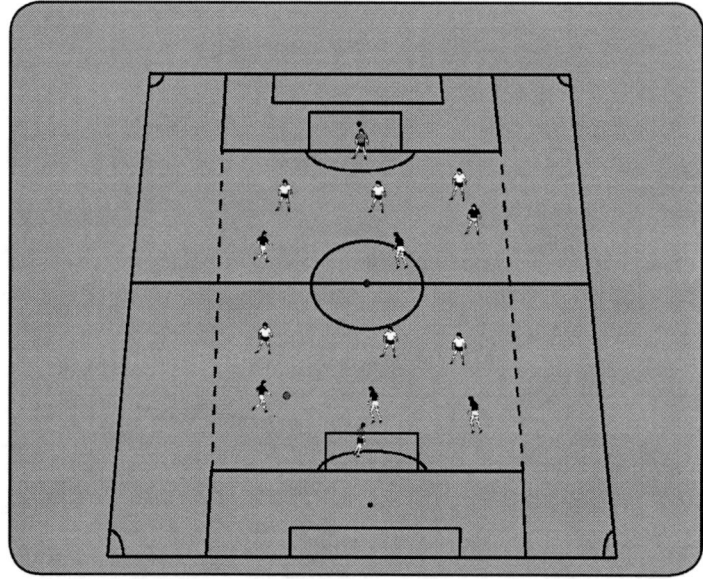

Contributed by long-time subscriber Gerry Canavan. In 2000, Gerry spent six weeks at Barnsley F.C. observing practices of all the teams and even training with the youth and reserve teams as well as helping to coach the younger Academy players. Gerry is an active coach (USSF "A" License and NSCAA Advanced Diploma) in his home town of Chicago where he is Director of Coaching for the Wilmette Wings S.C.

Organization: 10 v 10

The two teams must play between the offside lines (which can be coned or marked off). Both teams are shaped into a 4-3-2 formation with goalkeepers. The goalkeepers serve the ball in to the forwards to start play. If the combination play releases a player up the middle, then they have one touch to control and another touch to finish. (A one-touch finish is encouraged as the session progresses.) If the combination play releases a player out wide, then another player can run freely into the penalty area and score from the resulting cross.

Coaching Points

- Timing of the runs in behind the defense or across a defender is the key to success

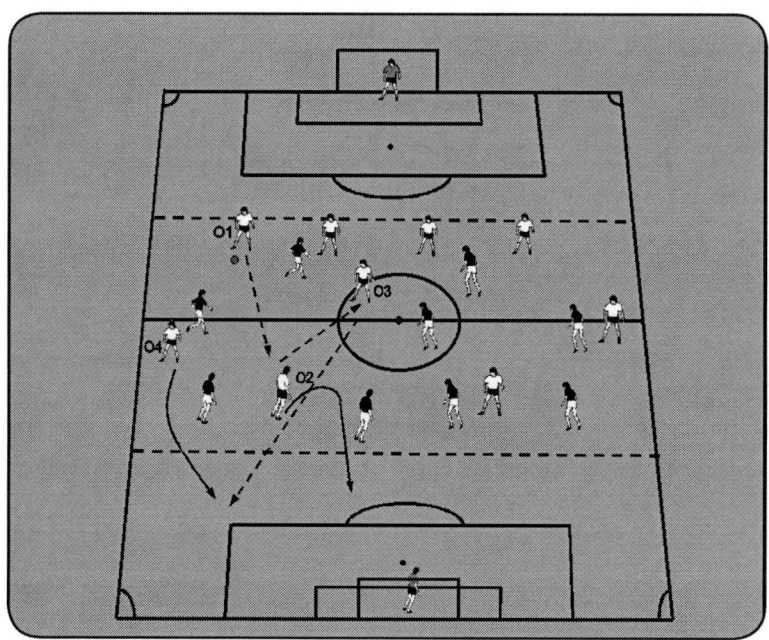

Chapter Eight

Games with Goals

Jeff Tipping is the National Director of Coaching Education for the NSCAA. This game is part of a session that was conducted at the WORLD CLASS COACHING International Coaching Seminar, February 20 - 22 at Arrowhead Stadium in Kansas City. The session focuses on small-sided games, specifically using 4 v 4 as a development tool.

4 v 4 Development

4 v 4 is widely recognized as the way to develop a young players understanding of the modern game. It has all aspects of playing forward, backward and sideways, plus all four players are always actively involved.

Using a 4 v 4 scenario with goalkeepers, the players form a diamond shape with players 4, 7, 11 and 9. In open play both teams are encouraged to "hit a pass" to player 9 (the center forward) as early as possible.

Coaching Points

Accuracy, pace, timing and the deception of the pass.

Rules

Long narrow field, kick-in's (no throw-in's) and for corner kicks, the team in possession's goalkeeper gets the ball.

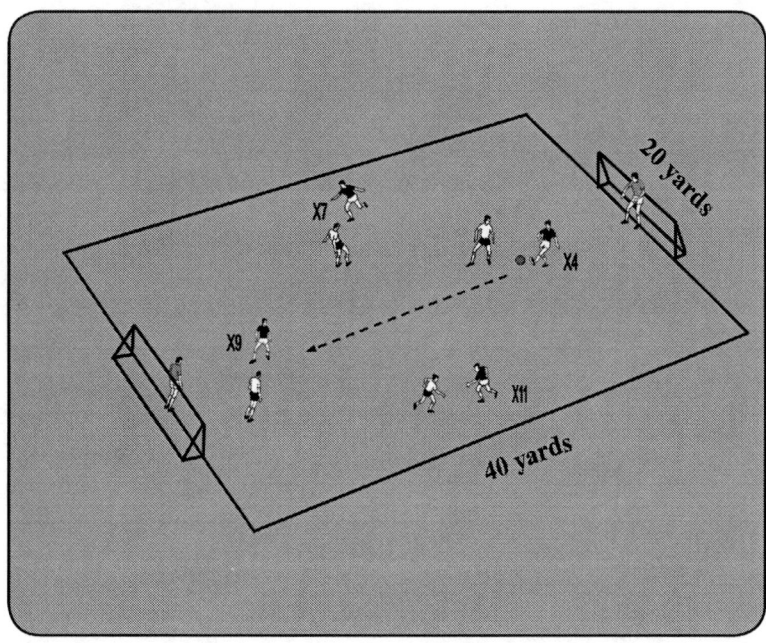

Visual Cues

Continuing with open play, the players are encouraged to work off visual cues directed by the coach:

- If X7 and X11 remain wide, they should try to feed X9
- If the white team covers the middle of the field as shown, the visual cue tells X4 to pass it wide
- If the white team spreads the field, then the opportunity to hit X9 quickly increases

Coaching Points

- Communication is essential
- Players to "go forward" at every opportunity. If they can't, then try to go sideways. The last resort is to go backwards

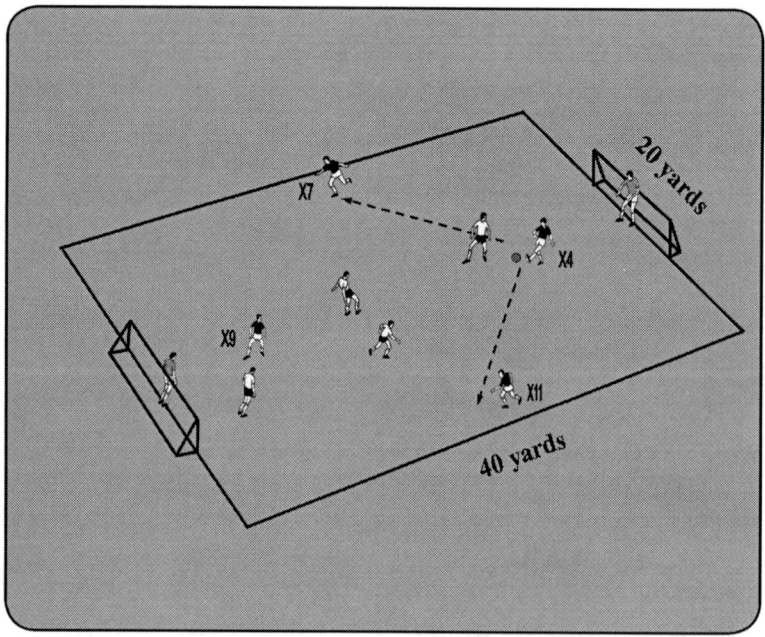

Progression to 5 v 5

X1, X2 and X3 play keep-away before playing a pass to X4 and X5 (targets), who hold play up before playing it back to either X1, 2 or 3. O1, O2 and O3 defenders are passive while O4 and O5 are active.

Visual Cues

Playing to the targets depends on the positioning of defenders O4 and O5.

Coaching Points

• Encourage being comfortable in possession
• Wide player's should "open up" when receiving passes so that they can see the 'forward' option

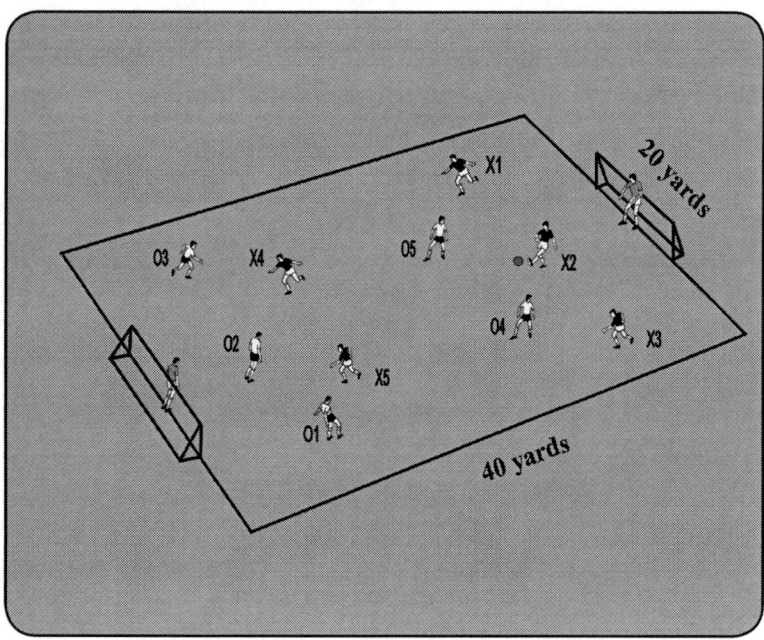

Live Game
Rules
If X's are in possession, O1, O2 or O3 becomes a second goalkeeper, leaving a
2 v 2 situation in X's attacking zone.

Progression
If X1, X2 or X3 plays a pass into the attacking zone, then they follow the pass
and create a 3 v 2 situation.

Progression
X1, X2 or X3 can dribble into the attacking zone to create a 3 v 2 situation.

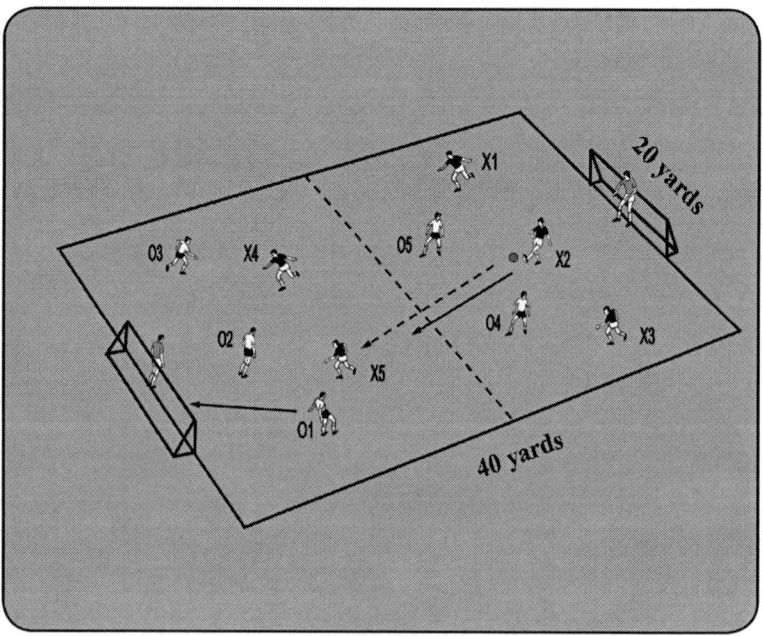

7 v 7 With Goalkeeper's

To finish the session, a 7 v 7 plus goalkeeper's game is set up with an emphasis placed on diamond shape creations using the shape and the visual cues that were encouraged in the small-sided games.

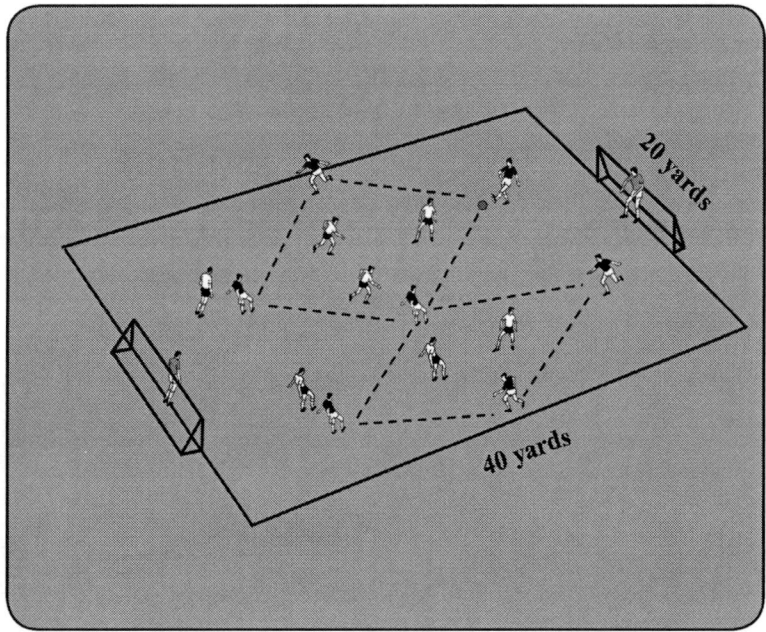

These games are from a session conducted at the February, 2004 WORLD CLASS COACHING International Coaching Seminar in Kansas City by John Murphy, then Assistant Coach of the Columbus Crew, John is the former goalkeeping coach with the New England Revolution and the session observed focuses on helping the goalkeeper deal with a back pass under pressure. The session was performed by the Under 16 Kansas City Legends.

Small-Sided Game: 6 v 5

To start the game, one goalkeeper throws the ball to the opposite goalkeeper. The receiving goalkeeper has two touches to control the ball and play it to a teammate and then the game is live. Following every save and re-start, the goalkeeper starts the game in the same fashion. The white team plays the game with (their team's) starting back four.

Coaching Points

- Goalkeepers are encouraged to play the longest pass possible
- Be prepared at all times, from both an attacker and defender

Progression

Goalkeepers aim the delivery to skip into the opposite goalkeepers feet. The defending team is encouraged to work the opponents forwards in terms of ball movement.

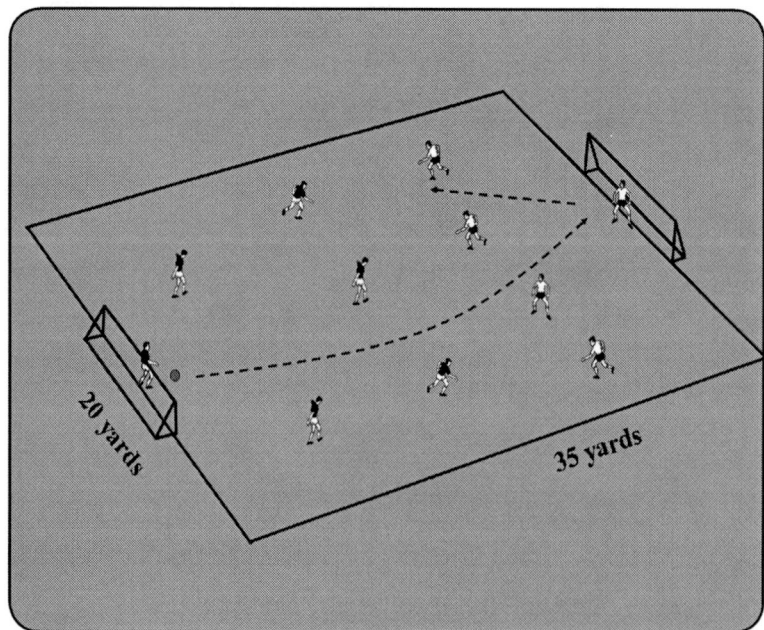

Small-Sided Game: "Box to Box": 8 v 8

End practice with a conditioned small-sided game. The teams can be split evenly or you could include one or more neutral players who always play for the team in possession. This gives the team with possession a numbers advantage enabling them to create more combination opportunities.

Conditioned small-sided games should encourage the players to put into effect what has been learned earlier in the practice. The conditions for this game are: goals can be scored only after your team has attempted a combination or each team earns a point following every successful combination.

The coach varies his delivery to the goalkeeper to start the game.

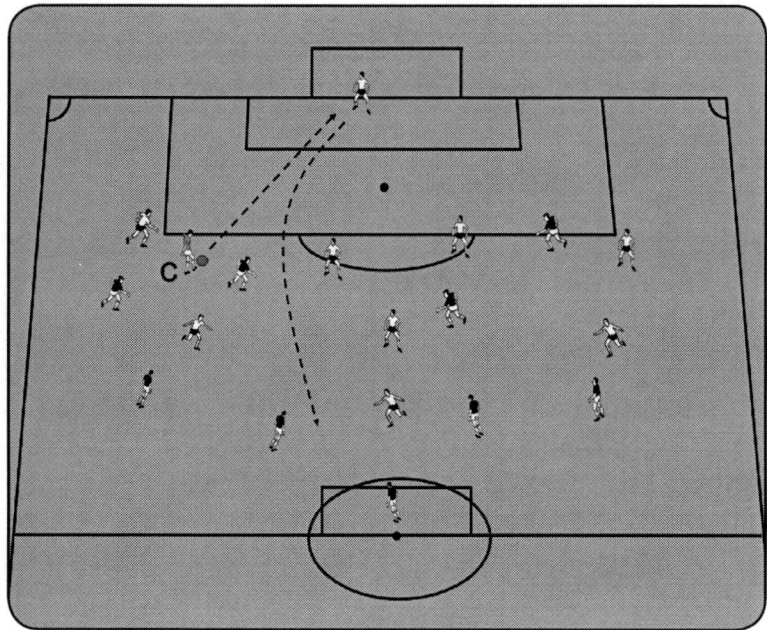

Contributed by Derek Broadley, former Academy Director at Crystal Palace F.C. of the English First Division and now National Director of Coaching for Premier Skills, a coach education company. Broadley is also the President of www.soccer-expert.com. This game in this session is geared toward young players from the ages of 8 to 12, but with an increased or decreased area size, can be used across different age ranges. This session can be seen in a video format at www.soccer-expert.com.

Activity Five: Staying with the ball

Using a field 60 x 40-yards with goals at either end, the group is split equally in number. Place gates around the wide areas of the field.

The objective is to play a regular game, with additional goals being awarded if a player can successfully run through a gate maintaining possession of the ball.

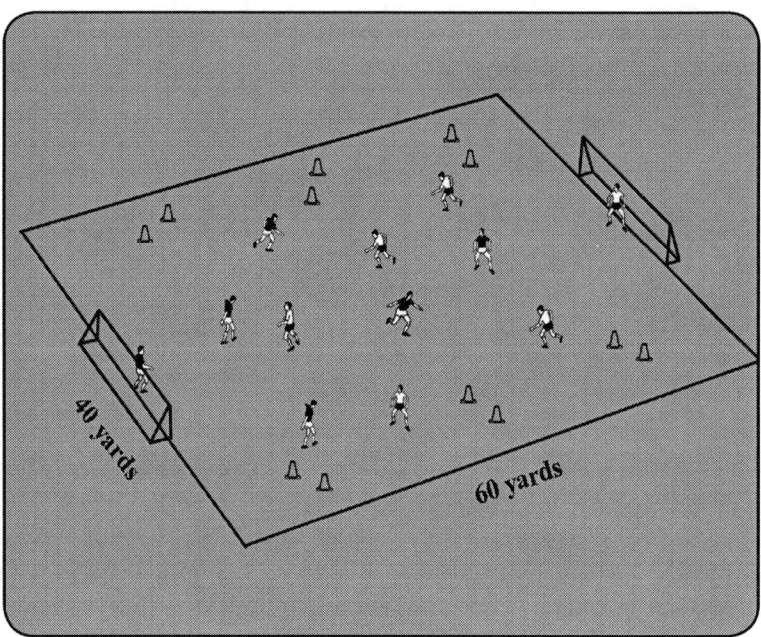

This game was part of a sessions that were observed by Daryn "Ozzie" White, Director of Coaching for Ankeny S.C. in Iowa, along with Sean Kehoe. Under the guidance of then manager Stuart Myrdoch, 1st team coach Jimmy Gilligan, Academy Director Martin Heather and Under 19's coach, Gary Smith, the following sessions were samples of the daily routine of some of the teams within the club.

5 v 5 + 1 with Target's

Using a 40 x 30-yard area, players play 5 v 5 + 1 to two small goals. Target players are now placed in each corner of the field and are allowed to move between cones, changing angles for receiving and returning passes.

Rules and Restrictions

The neutral player is restricted to one, two or unlimited touches. The target players are restricted to one touch. The 10 other players play two-touch. If a goal is scored in open play, one point is awarded, if a team scores after using a target player, three points are awarded.

Coaching Points

- Play forward quickly
- Penetrate early
- Support the ball as it travels
- Decision making

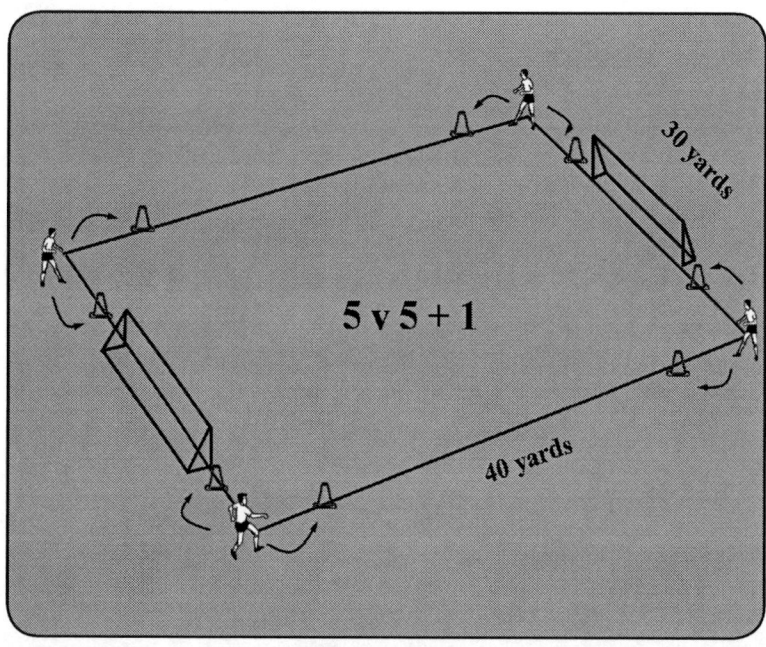

This game was part of a session observed October 5 in Kansas City.

Full-Field Game

Coach Tony DiCicco then spent 20 minutes working with the team with the following set-up. The field was set up with one goal on the edge of the penalty area as shown in diagram 10. The field was then split into three even sections. In one end, the three starting defenders played against the three starting forwards. In the middle third, the midfielders played 2 v 2 plus a neutral player that played for the team in possession. The other end had two defenders against two forwards. The players had to stay in their own third of the field except for a midfielder who could join the attacking third once the ball was passed in. The forwards could pass the ball back to a teammate into the middle third if they had no other options on offense.

Coach DiCicco would stop the game occasionally to get a point across, otherwise the players were allowed to play without restrictions.

The game progressed to a 7 v 7 + 1 game on the same field, except the field was narrowed both sides by five yards. Again, the starting forwards and starting defenders were on opposite teams.

Practice ended with the players having 15 minutes of free time to work on shooting, restarts, etc. Some players did sit-ups or spent their time stretching.

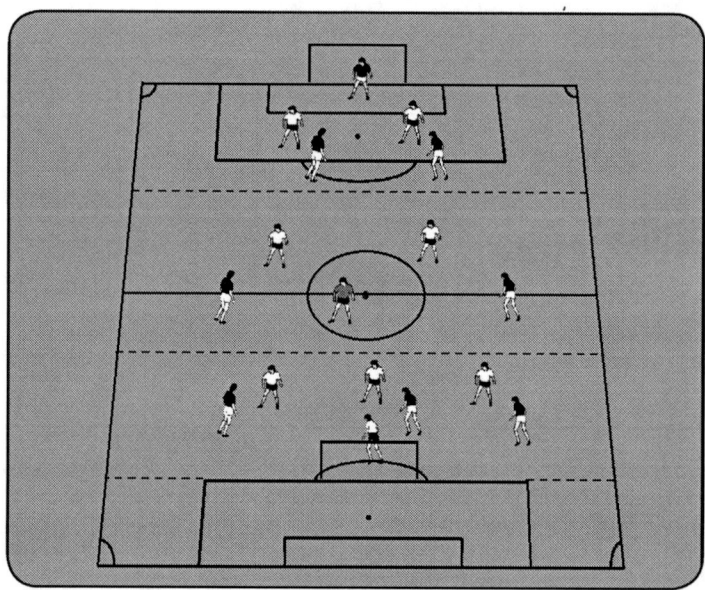

A finishing session contributed by then assistant coach of the Kansas City Wizards, Ken Fogarty.

Small-Sided Game
Organize the players into three teams of six and play 6 v 6 with goalkeepers and full-sized goals on a 20 x 30-yard field. The third team rests. The coach is on the perimeter of the field with a supply of balls and starts the game by serving a ball into the middle of the field. As balls go out-of-bounds, the coach continues to serve balls in to keep the game flowing. The first team to score three goals wins and the losing team is replaced by the third team waiting on the sidelines.

Coaching Points
• Quick decision making and finishing
• Accuracy over power
• Look for rebounds defensively and offensively

End practice with a cool down of jogging and stretching.

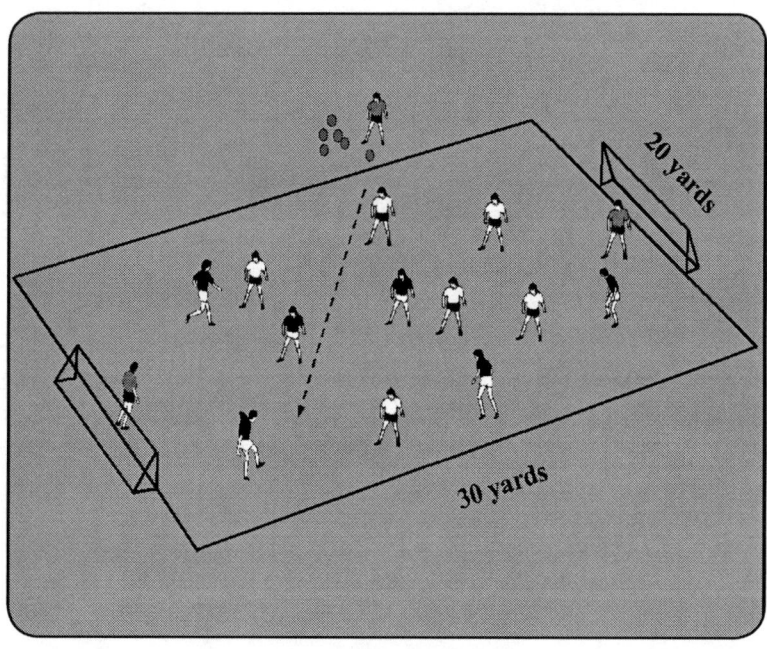

Chapter Nine

Miscellaneous

This game was part of a session conducted by Ian Currie at the Rangers F.C. Academy with the U12 team. The players were having a blast and loving every minute of this small-sided game

Four Goal Game

Place four small goals with goalkeepers on a 40 x 40-yard field. Organize four teams of three, with each team in a different color jersey. Each team is designated a goal to defend.

The objective is for the teams to play with each other (they can pass to any player from theirs or any other team) and attempt to score in any goal except the one they are defending.

When a team concedes a goal, they have to take a player off the field and play with just two players. Once another goal is scored, the player is allowed back on the field and replaced by a player from the team that has just conceded the goal.

Coaching Points
- Don't lose possession near your goal
- Look for longer passes away from your goal
- Change direction
- Shoot early and often

Observations
- The players absolutely loved this game and played with incredible enthusiasm
- There was lots of communication
- As the session progressed, more shots were taken

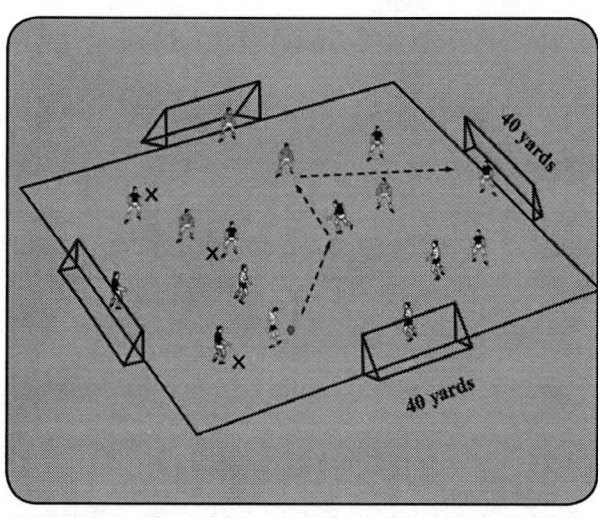

These games are part of a session contributed by Mike Matkovic the director of coaching for the Chicago Magic Soccer Club. Mike is a U.S.S.F. National Staff Coach, holds a USSF 'A' License and is the head coach of the USYSA Region Two '83 team. The Chicago Magic U16 Boys have been Illinois State Cup Champions at U12, U13, U15, and U16. They were Region Two semi-finalist in 1998 and Region Two champions in 1999 which they then followed with the USYSA Snickers National Championship later that same year.

Four Goal Game

Play from penalty area to penalty area with cones marking two small goals at both sides of the penalty areas. Play 8 v 8 plus two neutral players that play for the team in possession. Usually the two neutral players are our goalkeepers and they are allowed to use their hands. Shape the team in a 3-3-2 formation and have offside in effect. Place balls around the field to keep play moving. Play three 5-minute games - unlimited touches, two touch and unlimited touches.

Coaching Points
- Defensively - stay compact, when to press and when drop off
- Offensively - switch the point of attack, quick play, when to play around v when to get behind
- Transition - where to play the first pass

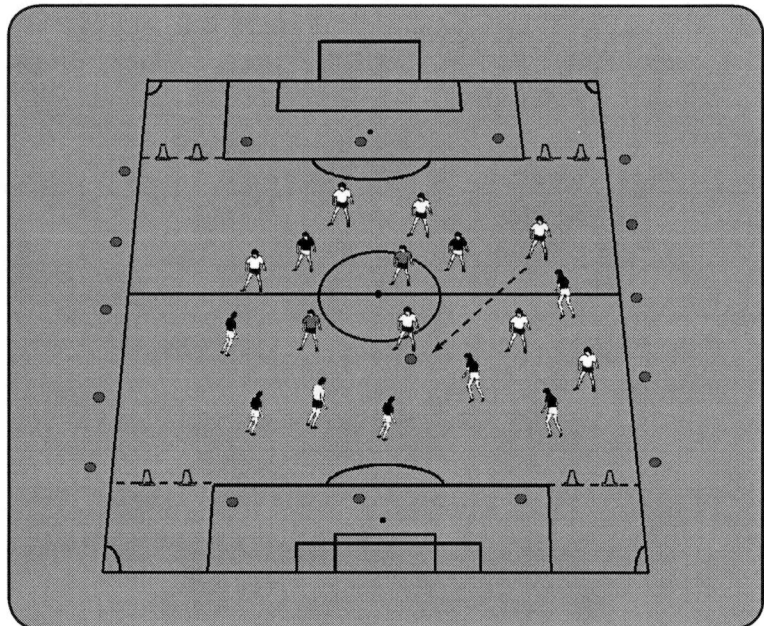

Progression
Progress into using goalkeepers in full size goals on the same size field and playing 8 v 8.

Coaching Points
Now is the time to get across all the previous coaching points in a more realistic game format.

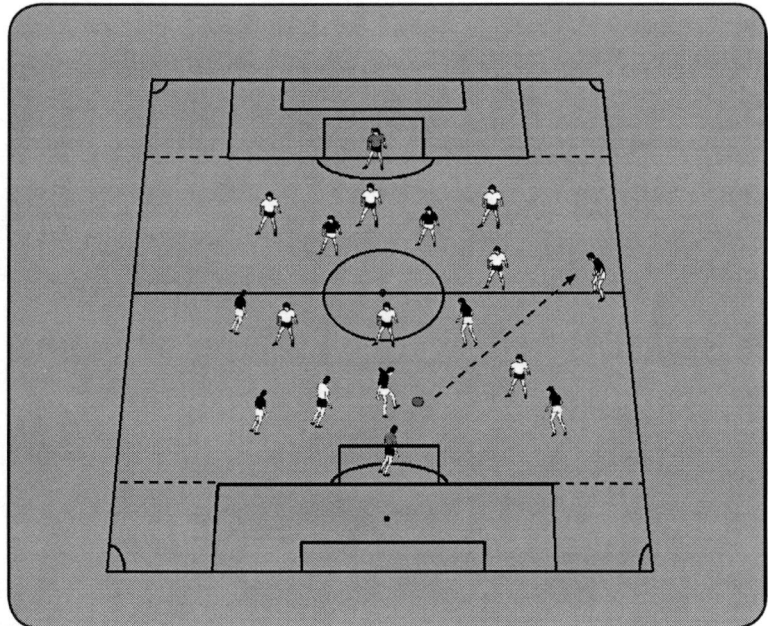

This game is part of a session that David Williams conducted at the WORLD CLASS COACHING International Coaching Seminar, Connecticut, June 2000, that included various exercises focusing on technique development for youth players. All the exercises can be used as warm-ups for just about any practice or they could be included as part of a typical training session to improve techniques.

Small-Sided Game

In a 40 x 30-yard area, play 5 v 5 with a target man on each end line. Score by passing from your own half to a target player on the end-line.

Coaching Points

• Only make the pass if it's on, do not force the long pass
• Keep possession until the pass is on
• Use the same turns and receiving techniques practiced in the previous drills.

Progression

Play with man-for-man markers. The aim is to lose your marker. Give one point if the players can perform a receiving technique practiced in the earlier exercises.

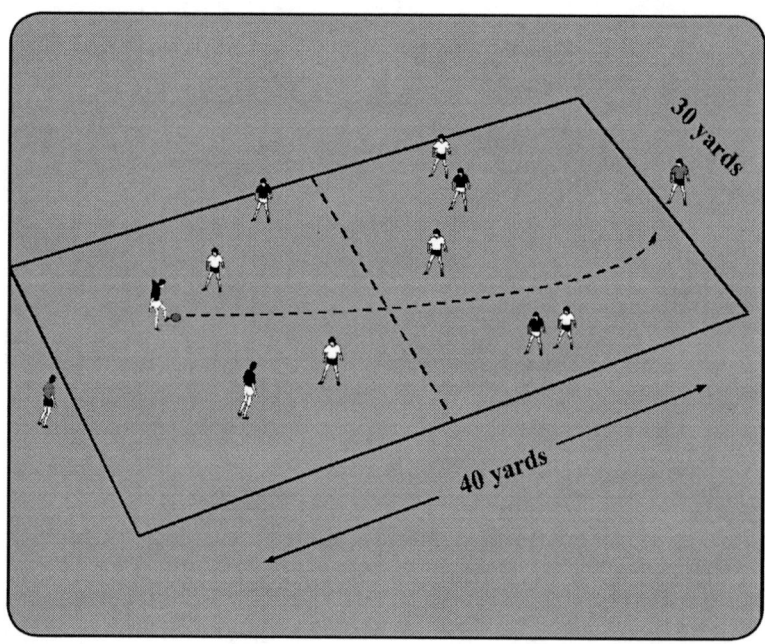

NEW - Bill Beswick's MasterCoach DVDs

New from Bill Beswick at Sportsmind - MasterCoach DVDs! This new series of DVDs gives coaches and players valuable insights into applied sports psychology topics – practical strategies that help to give competitive advantage and bring winning performances.

These DVDs are a great interactive tool for coach development in both professional and recreational sports – especially team sports and particularly soccer – at whatever age, ability or competitive level you operate.

Bill Beswick has been the sports psychologist at Manchester United, Derby County, Middlesborough and for the England National Team.

$34.95

Bill Beswick's MasterCoach 1

In typical style, Bill emphasises key principles and supports his points with anecdotes, case studies and fascinating film clips. Over an hour long overall, you can go to each 'chapter' from the Title Menu screen and this makes the DVD great in sections as stimulus material for discussions with groups of coaches, players, students or parents of young players to give better understanding of how psychology can influence and improve performance.

$34.95

Bill Beswick's MasterCoach 2

This DVD features two experts; England Soccer Team Psychologist Bill Beswick and Middlesbrough, English Premier League, goalkeeping coach Paul Barron. Together, they examine goalkeeping talent.

Elements of the complete goalkeeper are identified in key points using film clips from recent English Premier League games while a special feature in the technical skills section is a condensed 20 minute training session with Paul Barron and the Middlesbrough goalkeepers.